TWAYNE'S WORLD AUTHORS SERIES

A Survey of the World's Literature

ICELAND

Leif Sjöberg

State University of New York at Stony Brook

EDITOR

Snorri Sturluson

TWAS 493

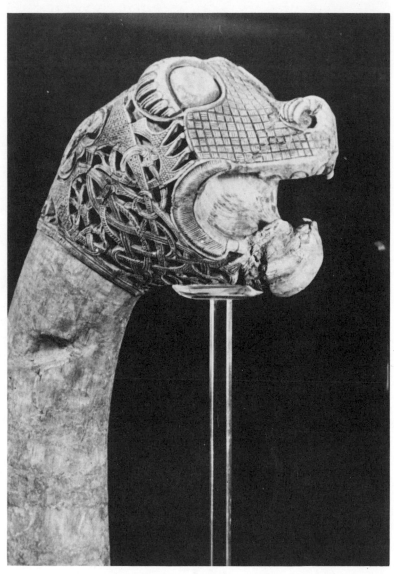

Protective Spirit, Oseburg Ship Burial

SNORRI STURLUSON

By MARLENE CIKLAMINI

Rutgers University
The State University of New Jersey

TWAYNE PUBLISHERS
A DIVISION OF G. K. HALL & CO., BOSTON

Published in 1978 by Twayne Publishers,
A Division of G. K. Hall & Co.
All Rights Reserved

Printed on permanent/durable acid-free paper and bound
in the United States of America

First Printing

Library of Congress Cataloging in Publication Data

Ciklamini, Marlene.
Snorri Sturluson.

(Twayne's world authors series ; TWAS 493 :
Iceland)
Bibliography: pp. 179–84
Includes index.
1. Snorri Sturluson, 1179?–1241—Criticism and
interpretation.
PT7335.Z5C5   839′.6′1   78–6624
ISBN 0–8057–6334–1

To the memory of Konstantin Reichardt

Contents

About the Author

Marlene Ciklamini is Professor and Chairman of the Department of German at Douglass College of Rutgers University where she has been teaching since 1959. As a member of the graduate School faculty, she teaches courses on Old Norse Literature and mythology at Rutgers. Professor Ciklamini received her B.A. from Douglass in 1956 and then went on to Yale to receive her M.A. in 1958 and her Ph. D. in 1961.

Professor Ciklamini is a member of the Society for the Advancement of Scandinavian Study, the Medieval Academy of America, the Modern Language Association, the American Association of Teachers of German and the Publication Committee of the American Scandinavian Society and has been listed in the 1971 edition of *Répertoire International des Médiévistes.* Her previous publications have dealt with the literary interpretation of sagas, prose works which encompass a wide variety of subject matter, the history of Norwegian kings, lives of Icelandic chieftains and poets, heroic legends, and Saint Lives.

Preface

Snorri's literary reputation rests primarily on his historic chronicle, *Heimskringla*, "*Sagas of the Norwegian Kings*," and to a lesser extent on the charmingly told myths in his mythological handbook, the *Prose Edda*. Despite the recognition that Snorri is one of the most imaginative, resourceful, and skilled writers of the Middle Ages, there is no literary analysis of his work in English except for discrete studies in handbooks and journals necessarily limited in scope or in approach.

In general, studies devoted to Snorri's work have had a utilitarian rather than an esthetic objective. Scholars have investigated the historicity of *Heimskringla* and have traced the transmission of narrative motives Snorri had culled from earlier sources, both extant and lost. There have been some signal exceptions, works by Sigurður Nordal, Hallvard Lie, and Siegfried Beyschlag, whose investigations are distinguished by a wider and inspiring purview. No single monograph written in recent years surpasses in depth of learning, literary observation, and broad interest the studies written by Nordal and Lie in the 1920s and 1930s.

Snorri's repute as a foremost author of the Middle Ages is hence beyond dispute. What is open to question are his reliability as a historian and the relationship of his works not to indigenous literary tradition but to medieval European culture as a whole. Snorri's presentation of Norway's history is deliberately realistic and seemingly objective. Character motivation in *Heimskringla* and the interplay of historic forces are revealed sharply and meticulously. Chronological relationships are handled with care according to traditional literary custom rather than by exact dating. Snorri's exacting craftsmanship and sound historical sense have consequently been a source of scholarly frustration and admiration which has tempted scholars to be preoccupied with separating fact from dissimulated fiction.

Concomitantly little attention has been given to the structure and unity of Snorri's work. In particular Snorri's concern with the mysterious interplay of a governing moral force and personal luck has been hardly explored. Yet Snorri's moral concern and his interest in the powerful role of luck in human destiny and stature interlink and structure the sagas in *Heimskringla*. Snorri, of course, is not a conventional moralist. There is no overt moralizing. Evildoers are not immediately punished. There is even a basic recognition that inhumanity is made to serve God's ends. Nevertheless, the existence of a moral force exacting retribution for transgressions against God's law is palpable in the presentation and marshaling of historic events.

The fate of Óláfr the Saint seems paradigmatic. He was victorious in the conquest of his kingdom and effective in the early years of his reign because he had carefully and consciously curbed his innate arrogance and cruelty. He loses control over his destiny when he imposes no restraint on the very qualities which had enabled him to fulfill his mission as Norway's missionary king. Personal luck seems hence dependent not only on the force of circumstance, on attainments and endowments, but also on the avoidance of excess, especially in the deployment of characteristics which had been essential for worldly success.

Snorri's preoccupation with moral questions links him to the intellectual milieu of medieval Europe. His reticence in explicating moral issues verbally, his avoidance of direct references or appellations to the divine except when mandated by historic events disclose his debt to native literary tradition. In his literary style as well as in his personal life Snorri was deeply aware of two modes of existence: the moral and spiritual concern of a Christian and the secular life of a chieftain. Whereas he failed in his life to reconcile the moral and secular demands imposed upon him, the secular and spiritual are in *Heimskringla*, his major literary work, adroitly and unobtrusively interwined.

Acknowledgments

I should like to thank my mother and my husband for their selfless help and encouragement. I should also like to express my gratitude to the Rutgers University Research Council for the generous support given me over the years. I am indebted to the Rutgers University Library staff; to Mr. Francis Johns, for building an Old Norse collection at the Alexander Library; and to the members of the interlibrary loan service, particularly to Mrs. Hedy Seitz for her unstinting kindness, energy, and resourcefulness, and to former librarians of the department, Mr. G. Kelley and Mr. R. Mulligan.

Chronology

1178 or   Snorri Sturluson born.
1179

1181   Fostered at age three by Jón Loptsson, the most powerful chieftain of Iceland.

1183   Snorri's father, Sturla (1115–1183), dies.

1197   Snorri's foster-father, Jón Loptsson, dies.

1199   Marries Herdís, the daughter of Bersi the Rich. They
separate later.

1201   Moves to the famous sagastead Borg, the ancestral
farm of the ninth-century poet and viking Egill Skallagrímsson.

1206   Moves to the glamorous and renowned sagastead Reykjaholt. Snorri administers several *goðorð*, "thing-districts," and parts of other thing-districts.

1215   Begins his first term as lawspeaker.

1218   End of first term as lawspeaker. Sails for Norway and
stays with Jarl Skúli in Túnsberg.

1219   Spring, travels to Gotland to visit Kristín, former widow
of Jarl Hákon galinn and wife of Swedish lawman
Áskell.

1219–   Winter, stays with Jarl Skúli in Trondheim.
1220

1220   King Hákon Hákonarson and his regent Jarl Skúli ap-
point Snorri *lendrmaðr*, "baron." Returns to Iceland.

1222–   Writes the *Prose Edda*. Composes first the last part,
1223(?) "Háttatal," a poem and text elucidating numerous skaldic
meters and poetical conventions. The poem is in honor
of Jarl Skúli and King Hákon Hákonarson.

1220–   Writes *Heimskringla, "The Sagas of the Norwegian
1235   Kings."*

1222–   Second term as lawspeaker.
1231

1224 Sets up house with Hallveig Ormsdóttir, the wealthiest woman in Iceland.

1227 Snorri and his brother Þórðr deprive their nephew Sturla Sighvatsson of the administration of the family thing-district.

1231 Snorri's son, Jón murtr, is slain in Norway.

1235 Snorri's son Óraekja raids the district known as Vest-firðingafjórðungr, a district controlled by his cousin Sturla Sighvatsson.

1236 Sturla Sighvatsson attacks Snorri. Sturla has Óraekja maimed. Snorri loses his power and lands to his nephew Sturla Sighvatsson.

1237 Sails to Norway. Stays in Trondheim, first with Jarl Skúli's son Pétr and then with Jarl Skúli.

1238 Sturla Sighvatsson is slain.

1239 Snorri returns to Iceland in defiance of the king's sailing ban.

1241 Snorri's wife, Hallveig, dies. September 22, Snorri is slain at the behest of Gizurr Þorvaldsson, his former son-in-law, and with the connivance of Hákon Hákonarson, the Norwegian king.

CHAPTER 1

Snorri, Poet and Chieftain:
An Ambivalent and Elusive Portrait

I Snorri's Stature as Writer and Poet

SNORRI STURLUSON (1178 or 1179 to 1241) is universally recognized as one of the great writers not only of Iceland but also of medieval Europe. His major works are the *Prose Edda,* a poetical handbook and repository of myths and heroic tales, and *Heimskringla,* a chronological series of sagas on the Norwegian kings. *Heimskringla* and parts of the *Prose Edda* are masterpieces of prose as well as invaluable sources of mythological lore and historical traditions.

As a poet Snorri has received less acclaim. Few of the poems which he composed for his preferment at the Norwegian court and for literary fame have been preserved.[1] As is often the case, Snorri's interpretative gift overshadowed his poetic ability. He was a brilliant interpreter of skaldic poetry, an indigenous Scandinavian form of verse, but only a minor practitioner of the art. Skaldic poetry was, however, of paramount importance to Snorri as a writer. His conversance with the poems extant in his time was one of the wellsprings of his work. To him the literary excellence of skaldic poems meant more than enjoyment. Since his contemporaries found it increasingly difficult to understand skaldic poetry and to master its essentials, he sought to assure its survival. He therefore set down and explained in his *Prose Edda* the complex meters of skaldic poetry and its metaphoric conventions. For Snorri, skaldic poems were also signal historical sources, for many were composed by court poets contemporary to the events commemorated and conscious of their obligation to uphold historic veracity.[2] Accordingly he cited skaldic verses to buttress his saga accounts

15

with trustworthy source material and coincidentally preserved some of the most brilliant and historically important poems of the Viking and post-Viking eras.[3]

The sense of irony and of precariousness which pervades Snorri's life is palpable also in the haphazard manner in which knowledge of Snorri's authorship was kept alive. Remembrance of Snorri as an author of note depended upon erratic scribal practices, since there was little interest in transmitting the names of authors of imaginative works. Unlike skalds, writers did not author original works, but solely reshaped traditional story matter. Evidently Snorri was honored by his contemporaries for his literary distinction. Yet his name appears only in one of the four principal manuscripts of the *Prose Edda,* the *Codex Uppsaliensis,* and does not occur at all in the extant medieval manuscript and manuscript fragments of *Heimskringla.* Only one complete and a partial translation of *Heimskringla* dating from the sixteenth century record his name.[4] Nevertheless, no scholar would seriously doubt that Snorri wrote *Heimskringla.* The consensus is that the transmission of Snorri's name as the author of *Heimskringla* was oral. *Sagas of Kings,* even though reshaped by a gifted writer of Snorri's stature, were communal works to be recited to an audience rather than read in the quietude of a cell or a secluded corner in the hall of an Icelandic farmstead.

The *Prose Edda* and *Heimskringla* are universally attributed to Snorri. Yet the question dogging scholars is whether Snorri may have written another saga of high artistic merit and historic interest, *Egils saga Skallagrímssonar,* a saga about an Icelandic Viking and skald. The evidence cited is circumstantial, but very suggestive. Snorri was a descendant of Egill. Like Egill he was chieftain and skald. Snorri, as a young chieftain, lived for several years (1201–1206) at Borg, Egill's ancestral farm. At this time, centuries after his death, Egill was still an active ancestor figure. Appearing in a dream Egill attempted to foil Snorri's departure to another farm by warning a descendant about the dire effects of the move.

The recurrent question cannot be put to rest: is it probable that Snorri's kinship to Egill and his residence at Borg inspired the saga of Egill, a man both akin and alien to Snorri

in character and outlook?[5] The answer, a tentative yes, is
based solely on conjecture. There was much to stimulate Snorri:
vivid traditions about Egill at Borg, the historical matter em-
bedded in the narrative matter, and the fascination exerted by
the complex and contradictory character of Egill who, unlike
Snorri, successfully joined the callings of a warrior and poet.
Egill's adventurous life would seem to invite the fashioning of
historic portraits. His background and exploits also lent themselves to presenting the periodic conflicts between the Norwegian
kings and chieftains with the cosmopolitan approach and un-
faltering objectivity characteristic of Snorri's mature work.

II *A Contemporary View of Snorri's Life and Character*

Even in his own time Snorri Sturluson was a respected though
enigmatic figure. To us the record of his life is clear in its
outlines, yet hazy in many aspects of his personal life, his role
as a chieftain, and in particular his development into a consummate writer.[6] Except for scattered notices of Snorri's activities,
there is only one relatively detailed contemporary account of
Snorri's character and actions, and this account is highly
ambivalent. Its author was Snorri's nephew, Sturla Þórðarson
(1214–1284),[7] himself a noted historian and sought-after saga-
teller.[8]

Sturla described his uncle's role and stature in his *Saga of
the Icelanders,* a panoramic work on the contemporary internecine and factious struggles for power. He was well qualified
for his task. He knew Snorri well. For a time he had lived
with Snorri, learning perhaps from Snorri the craft of composing
sagas. As a member of the powerful but fractious family known
as the Sturlungs, Sturla was involved at an early age in the
web of injustice, shifting allegiances, and uncontrollable, fateful
events. He was therefore both a historian of his own time and a
participant or witness of many of the deeds he recorded.

The Saga of the Icelanders is a difficult work to read. There
are scores of participants in a multitude of events from which
few guiding literary principles can be isolated. We conceive
respect, however, for Sturla's passion for detail and historic
veracity as well as sympathy for a man who, despite his usually

dispassionate style, conveys a sense of human impotence. The society Sturla described was rent by civil unrest and bloodshed. Even the most powerful leaders, ruled as they were by their passions, were frequently unable to mold events. Two lines in a contemporary verse preserved in the saga express the hopelessness implicit throughout the work: "Wound will requite wound . . . each savage assault will breed another."[9]

The feeling of impotence also structures Sturla's account of Snorri's life, although at first reading the densely woven texture of the saga inhibits an immediate grasp of this compositional design. Snorri is but one of the major figures in the convulsive struggles which preceded the death of the republic and heralded Iceland's subjection to the Norwegian crown in 1264. The compositional design becomes clear, however, when one isolates the statements on and references to Snorri from the interwoven strands of the narrative. Sturla's seemingly noncommittal account uncovers the serious flaws in Snorri's character, flaws which vitiated his life as a chieftain and which prevented him from attaining a position of preeminent leadership in Iceland's political affairs. In spite of his secular ambition Snorri could not direct some of the most crucial events of his life. At important junctures, the aspirations and willfullness of his followers and his own failings ensnarled him in decisions which contributed to his downfall and ultimately led to his violent death.

This structuring of Snorri's life as the life of a man whose great promise was unfulfilled is vexing to modern readers, partly because of Snorri's acknowledged brilliance as a writer and partly because of the incompleteness of Sturla's account. We sense or conjecture that an unsympathetic attitude toward Snorri might be responsible for the curious lacunae in Sturla's work. We hear, for instance, little of Snorri's boyhood and of his activities as a developing and mature author. He is rarely depicted as a man of charm, wit, and imagination,—the man, in short, we sense through his writings. Instead, we see a man totally engaged in accumulating power and wealth. The fault lies not in Sturla's poor craftsmanship as a writer. Sturla's sympathetic characterizations of his uncle Sighvatr and of Gizurr, his kinsman by marriage, disprove this assumption.

III   *Childhood and Youth*

In our age a writer's childhood and boyhood are of intrinsic interest. Invariably questions arise on how major experiences in a writer's formative years might have influenced or determined the style and subject matter of his works. These questions are also vital for an assessment of Snorri's intellectual and spiritual development. Sturla, however, provides only the bare essentials. He tells us that Snorri was fostered as a child by the most eminent man in Iceland, Jón Loptsson.

Snorri was born into the family of an upstart chieftain.[10] His father, Sturla (d. 1183), had achieved prominence by skillfully exploiting lawsuits. In medieval Iceland litigation was a traditional way to maintain and expand power. Knowledge of the law, skill in arbitration on the thing, a judicial assembly, and relentless prosecution of lawsuits, by force if necessary, led to a tangible increase in power. The increase in power was predicated upon a legally sanctioned weakening of adversaries by the imposition of fines and by discrete forms of outlawry through which the prosecuted could be outlawed from the district or the country for a specified number of years or for life. Since thingmen tended to ally themselves with the powerful chieftain within their district, hoping that he would best serve their interests, successful litigation meant more than the acquisition of prestige. Indeed, by the vigorous pursuit of his lawsuits, Sturla had laid the foundation for his descendants' political prominence in the first part of the thirteenth century, an era aptly named the Age of the Sturlungs.

Snorri's father reached the pinnacle of success when Snorri was three, the age when a child's consciousness of the world around him expands. Jón Loptsson, the most powerful man of Iceland, offered to foster Snorri as part of a legal settlement Jón had been asked to arbitrate. The system of fosterage was traditional in Iceland, yet is implied in most fosterage cases that the foster father (by the act of fosterage) acknowledged the superiority of the man whose child he fostered. Jón's position was too unassailable to allow the traditional interpretation of fosterage. His fosterage of Snorri was rather a gesture of magnanimity which signaled the stature Sturla had attained.

The bonds of fosterage were usually strong. In Snorri's case,

the fosterage, we surmise, had a particularly formative impact on
the development of Snorri's intellect and attitudes. Jón was,
as the sources agree, the greatest chieftain in Iceland. He was
by all accounts a strong-willed but wise man. He would not
allow himself to be cowed even under threat of excommunica-
tion.[11] Jón's preeminence was based not only on his indisputable
power but rested also on his learning and wealth. His household
at Oddi was the center of ecclesiastical and worldly learning
and was renowned for its munificence and splendor.[12]

The tradition of learning had been strong at Oddi for several
generations and Jón upheld this tradition. His grandfather,
Sæmundr the Learned (d. 1133), had studied in Paris and was
famed for his wisdom and scholarship. He was the first historian
of the Norwegian kings and his knowledge inspired so much
awe that, like the poet Virgil in medieval belief, Sæmundr was
fictionalized as a sorcerer.[13] Sæmundr, a priest by training,
transmitted his love for knowledge to his descendants. One of
his sons, Eyjólfr, established a school at Oddi. Jón himself was
trained as a deacon and was considered a most knowledgeable
man in ecclesiastical matters. This acknowledgment of Jón's intellectual stature was not an instance of fulsome praise, but a
sober assessment recorded in a saga on Jón's bitter enemy, Bishop
Þorlákr, one of the early Icelandic saints.

Great minds are often nurtured by great teaching. That Jón
fostered the tradition of learning is palpable in the high standards of Snorri's works and also in the intellectual attainments of
Jón's son Páll, later a bishop. Of Páll it was said that he was
learned at a young age, could write well, and was adept at
everything he did. He continued his education in England.
Upon his return Páll surpassed his contemporaries in the making
of verse, the writing of books, and the beauty of his singing.[14]
The training of men of Snorri's and Páll's intellectual distinction
testifies to the rigorous standards of learning upheld at Oddi.

Learning in medieval Iceland comprised not only ecclesiastical subjects, but also a sound knowledge of the law,
genealogies, the history of Norway (the ancestral land of many
Icelanders), stories and sagas about prominent Icelanders of the
past, and the art of skaldic poetry. Ecclesiastical learning has
left little overt influence on Snorri's writings, but his thorough

training in the laws of Iceland is evident in his election as law-speaker in 1215 and later in 1222. The office of lawspeaker was of importance in the governance of the island, for it was the law-speaker's function to recite the body of law at the opening of the thing and to act as interpreter in legal disputes. The office holder was expected to have total recall of the laws of the country. That Snorri held the office for a period of eleven or fifteen years (1215–18, 1222–31 or 35) attests the esteem accorded to Snorri's mastery of the law.

It is not surprising that the school at Oddi should teach law. Knowledge of the law was requisite in the education of boys who were to be trained as leaders. One of Jón Loptsson's illegitimate sons, Ormr Jónsson, was renowned for his legal learning, and Bishop Páll himself is credited with initiating a legal reform to prevent widespread fraud in measuring cloth. For holders of high church offices a thorough knowledge of the island's laws was prized. Bishop Klængr (d. 1176), for instance, received high praise for his command of secular law. The litigant whom the bishop supported, his saga states, invariably won his case. Perhaps the most important testimony to the necessity of teaching law is the fact that laws, in addition to genealogies and ecclesiastical writings, were the earliest works to be committed to writing.[15]

Learning laws and genealogies in medieval Iceland generated an interest in history. Laws were considered a treasured heritage and any infringement was not lightly brooked. "This country shall be governed by law" is an almost proverbial expression in the sagas. Laws were transmitted from generation to generation, altered only when changing social conditions necessitated amendments to individual laws or to the jurisdictional system. The circumstances which induced changes in laws or legal procedure were hence historical events to be committed to memory. Similarly the upholding of the law or its disregard by Scandinavian kings were among the recorded facts of their reigns. Knowledge of genealogies was of equal importance in an aristocratic society in which social position was determined by birth and achievement. A man's claim to fame and stature rested not only on his accomplishments, but also on the renown of his ancestors. Consequently saga heroes normally have distinguished forebears.

Snorri's stature as a historian is rooted almost certainly in the teaching he received at Oddi. The learning of laws and genealogies required a devotion to accurate transmission of knowledge. But he also acquired an interest in contemporary events and particularly in the interconnections between Iceland and Norway, between Icelanders and the Norwegian kings and their chieftains. Jón had spent some time at the Norwegian court. His mother was an illegitimate daughter of King Magnús Bareleg. She was recognized as a member of the royal family in Jón's presence during the crowning of King Magnús Erlingsson by the papal legate Stephen in 1163. Jón spoke of this momentous event, as Snorri relates in *Heimskringla*. Jón's eyewitness accounts probably deepened Snorri's respect for truth in historical transmission, an intellectual standard which Snorri, as a mature historian, admired in the work of Ari Þorgilsson, the father of Icelandic historical writings, and in men of Ari's stature.[16]

Jón no doubt cherished his royal descent. Consonant with the traditions of the Norwegian kings and the powerful jarls of the Trondheim district Jón had his ancestry celebrated in a skaldic genealogical poem, "Nóregs konungatal."[17] The existence of this poem, which was probably recited to Jón at a festive occasion, suggests that Snorri learned the art of skaldic poetry at Oddi. The indirect evidence that Snorri received intensive instruction in skaldic poetry is persuasive. As all poets in an oral culture, Snorri must have had extensive training. He had to learn a complex system of versification and to acquire command of poetical figures rooted in pagan myths and heroic stories. Snorri himself was the descendant of major skalds, of Egill Skallagrímsson and Markús Skeggjason. Snorri's consciousness that he descended from illustrious skalds almost certainly matured his understanding and appreciation of the difficult craft. In any event, when we first encounter Snorri as a young and ambitious man, Snorri is an accomplished skald, proud of his talent as a poet and eager to employ his art to make himself known abroad. He sent, for instance, a poem to a powerful Norwegian chieftain, Hákon galinn (d. 1214), and received in return the magnificent gift of a sword, shield, and armor. Snorri's incorporation of skaldic verses in *Heimskringla* and in particular the writing of his *Edda* may be conceived as the fruit of the teaching he had received at Oddi. With the apprehension of a poet educated at a school at which book learning was prized, he felt compelled to commit to parchment the myths and heroic stories used in poetry and skaldic stanzas which illustrated poetic matter and distinct verse forms. He thus attempted to revive an ancient art which could survive no longer by oral transmission.

Saga telling flourished in thirteenth-century Iceland. On the large farmsteads, in an essentially aristocratic milieu, sagas were cultivated which related the exploits of hero ancestors who had settled the island. These sagas were called *Family Sagas*, and their settings were specific areas of the country. During the long winter nights and at festivals Snorri probably heard the sagas attached to Oddi and Hvamm, the farm owned by Snorri's father. The farm of Njáll, for instance, was in the vicinity of Oddi, and tales about the wisdom and craftiness of Njáll, a pagan with a Christian attitude toward the taking of life, circulated before the classical version of his saga was committed to writing. In addition to the pride of old aristocratic families in their heritage, reminders from Iceland's past also furthered saga telling. Snorri's mother, for example, was present when the body of Snorri goði, the hero of the *Eyrbyggja saga* and an ancestor of Snorri, was disinterred and transported to a new cemetery.[18] Such an event and the finding of old weapons spurred saga telling. Snorri's narrative power owes much to the dramatic techniques which are characteristic of the nonromantic saga style.

At Oddi then, Snorri developed into the man and writer we seem to know so intimately. The instruction he received there 1) prepared him for the prestigious office of lawspeaker, which he held twice in his life; 2) trained him as a skald and a historian; 3) taught him the elements of rhetoric and the art of saga telling. His upbringing at Oddi also influenced the type of life Snorri tried to create when he reached independence. Like his foster father, Jón, Snorri strove for undisputed eminence. He sought recognition at home and at the Norwegian court. He loved splendor as Jón did and displayed it, since munificence was both the symbol and the basis for power. He was also as uxorious as Jón. Snorri married twice, was separated from his first wife, had a series of concubines and a number of legitimate and illegitimate children.[19]

Despite the strong influence of Jón and of the intellectual life at Oddi on Snorri's development, Snorri is unmistakably a Sturlung. His consciousness of his illustrious ancestry was of signal importance. His paternal grandmother was related to Bishop Ketill (1122–1145). His great-grandmother descended from Snorri goði, one of the major saga figures. His mother, Guðný, Sturla's second wife, was the descendant of Egill Skalla-grímsson, the Viking warrior, about whom Snorri may have composed the brilliantly conceived *Egils saga Skallagrímssonar*. Markús Skeggjason, a noted lawspeaker and skald, was also one of Guðný's forebears. The accomplishment of Snorri's ancestors evidently nurtured his self-esteem and infused him with a belief in his own talent.

To his father Snorri and his brothers owed a composite of mental gifts and character traits, the most important of which were a drive for power, self-confidence and egotism, eloquence, and persuasion. Two of the brothers, Snorri and Sighvatr, inherited their articulateness and imaginative quickwittedness from Sturla. It was said that Sturla could spellbind an audience while reciting his legal involvements. Indeed, Sturla's detached irony at a moment of stress and apparent humiliation is reminiscent of the composure of saga heroes. Sturla, after a woman had slashed his chin during a legal embroilment, solely remarked that women had odd ways in searching for love.[20] Snorri's innate gift as a storyteller seems to have been essentially of the same cast as Sturla's except that the sphere of interest has shifted. Instead of concentrating on contemporary, self-centered issues within the narrow confines of one Icelandic locale, as Sturla had done, Snorri ventured into the realms of mythology and of the history of the Norwegian kings.

IV   Snorri's Accumulation of Wealth, Power, and Prestige

Wealth was the basis for a successful chieftaincy in thirteenth-century Iceland and had been so in the earlier heroic society Snorri knew so well from tales and poetry. Snorri, as a young man, lacked wealth. His mother had squandered his patrimony. Snorri hence lacked the means to establish himself in a society in which the number of followers and the acquisition of thing-districts (named *goðord*) were equal in importance to the mental and personal attributes required of an aspiring chieftain.

The principal task, as Snorri saw it, was the acquisition of wealth, and this task he accomplished well. With the aid of his brother Þórðr and Jón Loptsson's son he contracted a wealthy marriage. He married the future heiress of Bersi the Rich. Within a few years, after Bersi's death, he was able to move from Oddi to Borg, the farm Bersi had owned and some centuries back the homestead of the saga-hero Egill Skallagrímsson. Snorri was now a rich man, but his earlier financial straits may have had a far-reaching influence on his later life. At crucial periods of his life he exhibited an injudicious avarice, perhaps the result of years of financial dependency.

Snorri's ambition to be a great chieftain is revealed in the first purposeful acts of early adulthood. He strove to accumulate power by acquiring control over various thing-districts. Sturla shows Snorri at that period in an unfavorable light. Snorri, it seems, was willing to exploit enmities and cared little about questions of right and wrong in his quest for stature. This deviousness was a two-edged sword Snorri employed throughout his life. He was known to be fickle in his friendships and alliances and he fomented rivalry and hostility. Power was more important to him than friendship and kinship. Thus he failed to see the shortcomings inherent in pursuing power for the sake of power, failings he had seen so clearly in kings he had characterized in *Heimskringla*.

Acts of injustice, indifference toward the obligations of friendship and kinship, and the instigation of disputes illustrate Snorri's disregard for right and wrong. In a quarrel with a merchant from the Orkneys Snorri seized the flour the merchant had stored on Snorri's farm. The merchant had been Snorri's winter guest, a friend of his stepbrother, and a man who stood under the protection of Sæmundr, the son of Jón Loptsson. The sequel discloses Snorri's unscrupulous vindictiveness. After the merchant had slain one of Snorri's men, Snorri incited an unsuccessful attack on the merchant's ship. When the merchant sought refuge with Sæmundr, Snorri sent three hirelings to slay his prey. Throughout the incident Snorri ignored the feelings of his dying stepbrother and Sæmundr's friendship for the merchant's prominent uncle.

The aftermath to a confrontation at the thing also demonstrates Snorri's callousness toward Sæmundr. Magnús, Sæmundr's nephew, wounded his hand when he barehanded seized a sword in a fracas between his men and Snorri's. A precarious settlement was reached according to which Sæmundr was to impose the monetary fine he considered adequate for the injury. Snorri disliked the agreement intensely. He therefore initiated against Magnús a lawsuit which would divert attention from the settlement and weaken Magnús' social standing. Snorri's duplicity is as evident in the scheming of the divertive lawsuit as it is in the execution of the litigation. At issue was the estate of Magnús' thingwoman, who had died without leaving a legitimate heir. Snorri deprived Magnús of the inheritance by declaring a vagrant, whom Snorri's retainer had picked up in the South, the woman's legitimate heir. Snorri then took up the inheritance case and had Magnús outlawed. The settlement which followed the verdict increased Snorri's repute and power as a chieftain.

In these years which preceded Snorri's first journey to Norway, Snorri had firmly established his position of leadership despite an innate disinclination to participate in battles. We observe on two occasions that Snorri was loath to distinguish himself as a warrior. Once Snorri refused to break up a melee between two angry factions of his thingmen. He said he did not have a big enough force to control their stupidity. In another incident, an armed confrontation, Snorri defended his position only half-heartedly until his brothers came to his assistance. Snorri preferred to attain distinction by other means. He amassed a fortune, supervised profitable farms, used his legal knowledge for public advancement, and acquired control over important thing-districts. Despite his pennilessness at the outset of his career, Snorri achieved such prominence that his power was recognized outside of Iceland. A letter from the Norwegian archbishop addressed to Iceland chieftains lists Snorri as one of the leaders responsible for the political and social life on the island and thus for the well-being of the Church.[21]

Besides acquiring wealth and power, Snorri also sought to establish himself as a skald of distinction. Recognition as a

skald depended in large measure upon the fame achieved at
royal courts. For this reason Snorri set out to win renown as a
skald even before he sailed to the Norwegian court. He composed poems to King Sverrir (d. 1202), King Ingi Bárðarson
(d. 1217), the regent Jarl Hákon galinn (d. 1214), and Frú
Kristín, Hákon's consort. Ironically these efforts had only a
fleeting worldly success. All of the rulers honored had died before
Snorri left Iceland for the court. Frú Kristín was alive, but she
had married a prominent Swedish chieftain, the lawman of West-
gotland.

By sending these poems unsolicited to the rulers of Norway,
Snorri achieved nevertheless a limited objective. The munificent
gift Jarl Hákon sent Snorri as a princely reward for his poem
contributed to Snorri's reputation at home. The poem he had
sent to King Ingi Bárðarson probably accounts for the warmth
with which Jarl Skúli, Ingi's half-brother, welcomed Snorri at
court. Yet in a larger sense the honor Snorri had attained proved
to be ephemeral. He lacked the makings of a great skald, poetical
inspiration and the ability to be an honored but independent
member of the court.

We know little about Snorri's first stay in Norway. The few
facts we do learn suggest the force of Snorri's personality and a
strong desire for prominent involvement in political affairs. He
was lavished with honors. Jarl Skúli and the young King Hákon
honored him with the title of *skutilsveinn*, "page at the royal
table," and then made him a baron. In return, they charged him
with a dual mission: to settle grievous hostilities between Icelanders and Norwegian merchants and to bring Iceland under
Norwegian rule. By assuming this diplomatic task Snorri had
prevented an imminent invasion of Iceland and had thus postponed Norway's eventual control over the island.[22]

V   *An Elusive Quest to Consolidate Power*

After his return to Iceland in 1220 Snorri set out to consolidate
his power, but concomitantly and paradoxically unleashed the
forces which were to constrict his might and cause his death. His
arrival in Iceland highlights the animosity which would beset
his life. He rode to his farm in splendor with the spectacular gifts,

accoutrements, and personal polish acquired at the Norwegian court. At the same time he was met with suspicion and hostility. The kinsmen of Jón Loptsson, his foster father, charged him with complicity in the king's refusal to pay compensation for an unwarranted slaying: Ormr, a son of Jón, had been slain by a Norwegian merchant. The tension created by Snorri's display of the favor he had found at court and by the concomitant rumors was vented in a defaming, scurrilous verse of ridicule. Although scurrilous verses normally led to the immediate slaying of the originator, Snorri acted with deliberation. He exploited the resentment which a nephew of Jón Loptsson harbored against his adversary and incited him to do battle. In the attack, the battle of Breiðabolstað (1221), Snorri's enemy was slain. Symptomatic of the unstable and conflicting loyalties of the age was the defense of Snorri's adversary by a son-in-law and some of his friends.

The events surrounding the battle at Breiðabolstað offer insight into Snorri's handling of conflicts. Snorri avoided battles consistently. During the next two decades he would mass his troops occasionally to display his power rather than to mete out death. By design and good fortune he was never forced to commit his troops to battle. Snorri continued rather to press for power by fomenting hostilities, accumulating wealth and thing-districts, and arranging potentially advantageous marriages.

Snorri attained only one of his goals. He made himself the wealthiest man of Iceland. The control his foster father, Jón, had exerted over the affairs of the island eluded him, however. The marriages he arranged were, except for his own remarriage, singularly unhappy and were ultimately the cause of ill will. The hostilities he encouraged festered and finally weakened his position. The alliances he established were shortlived and shortsighted.

Marriages in medieval Iceland were contracted to strengthen alliances and to conclude hard-headed property agreements. The marriages of his three daughters were, however, singularly unhappy and his alliances with his sons-in-law were shortlived. The marriages of two daughters ended in divorce. The second marriage of his daughter Hallbera was also unhappy and brief. His daughter Þórdís was widowed and attracted lovers.

Property division upon the death of a marriage partner or upon divorce tended to stir discord and to inspire rancor. Two of Snorri's former sons-in-law harbored deep resentment. Árni, whom Snorri forced to cede the property of Brautarholt, was to have a fateful relationship to Snorri. As a trusted messenger of the Norwegian king, Árni delivered the royal letter authorizing Gizurr, also a former son-in-law, to seize Snorri and if necessary to slay him. Kolbeinn, Snorri's widowed son-in-law, also became one of the most determined foes of the Sturlungs. Despite a brief reconciliation Kolbeinn never forgot that Snorri had extracted from him half of a thing-district which rightfully belonged under his own control. Snorri's unwillingness to distribute his wife's inheritance to her stepsons in an equitable manner hastened the moment of his death. His stepsons had joined Gizurr by the time Gizurr ordered Snorri's death.

Snorri had hoped to augment his power by enflaming hostilities against rival chieftains. The long-range result, however, was the acerbating of animosity. His relations with Þorvaldr Vatnsfirðingr and his nephew Sturla Sighvatsson exemplify the complexities which attended the outbreak of strife. Þorvaldr was a powerful chieftain whose thing-district was close to Sturla Sighvatsson's territory. Sturla Sighvatsson was emerging as one of the strong men of the times. As usual, Snorri incensed smoldering hatred to harm Þorvaldr. Snorri incited such hatred in the kinsmen of a woman whom Þorvaldr's brother had seduced that they spearheaded repeated attacks upon Þorvaldr's life. The result was that Þorvaldr renounced his earlier friendship with Sturla, allied himself with Snorri, and married Snorri's daughter Þórdís. The strife, however, still persisted. Þórvaldr was eventually slain by old enemies, now supported by Sturla Sighvatsson, while Þorvaldr's sons by a concubine were killed in a subsequent raid led by Sturla.

Sturla's involvement in the slaying of Þorvaldr illustrates the acceleration and intensification of strife unwisely provoked. Sturla wanted to even the score among himself, Þorvaldr, and Snorri. Abetting the attack on Þorvaldr and securing shelter for the slayers expressed both his resentment at Þorvaldr's disloyalty and his anger that Snorri and his brother Þórðr had legally forced him to surrender the family's thing-district. The killing of Þorvaldr's sons had a different motive. They were slain in revenge for an attack on Sturla's farm.

Sturla's hatred repeatedly and imprudently provoked was to blight Snorri's life. By charging his unruly son Órækja with the governance of the thing-district once held by Þorvaldr, Snorri fanned Sturla's ire. The vicious outbreak of Sturla's resentment would be postponed, however, until Sturla's return from a pilgrimage to Rome and a subsequent stay at the Norwegian court. Consequently, Sturla's return from Norway as the emissary of the king (1235), entrusted with Iceland's submission to the Norwegian crown, marks a turning point in Snorri's life. Snorri's combativeness had lessened and his legal scheming had come to a halt. Sturla, in turn, had become more treacherous and implacable in his dealings with anyone he considered his foe. Shortly after Sturla had returned, he moved against Snorri and Órækja. He seized Snorri's farm, Reykjaholt, and in a sudden abrogation of a treaty, he had Órækja gelded and attempted to have him blinded. In spite of the damage to his property, the loss of the famous sagastead of Reykjaholt, and the mutilation of Órækja, Snorri planned no effective strategy to combat Sturla. He chose to conclude ineffective alliances, to muster and to mass troops and, if need be, evacuate farms he considered vulnerable to attack. Above all, he avoided face-to-face negotiations with Sturla, no doubt because of Sturla's maiming of Órækja during a truce.

Snorri's alliances at this time were ineffective. They were at best a means to buy time. His most prominent allies were Þorleifr Görðum, a kinsman who was perturbed by Órækja's mutilation, and Gizurr, a former son-in-law. Þorleifr's support was ineffective because Þorleifr had misjudged Sturla's implacability. Snorri and Þorleifr amassed troops for an assault on Sturla, but desisted from offering battle at Þorleifr's advice. Þorleifr believed that Sturla's force was superior to theirs and that they should enter into negotiations. Snorri's decision to leave with a single companion proved to be wise. Þorleifr was unable to agree to Sturla's terms and suffered total defeat. His farm was cruelly despoiled of livestock and he was forced to sail for Norway. For Snorri Þorleifr's defeat was a severe blow. Sturla, Snorri realized, could not be checked. Snorri's second and last journey to Norway followed the ill-fated attempt to curb Sturla's power.

Snorri's friendship with Gizurr amounted to little, though in retrospect Snorri's confidence in Gizurr seems singularly misplaced. Gizurr was to be the Sturlungs' most formidable foe. He broke the power of the Sturlungs in a ferocious battle. Then he decided to kill Sturla himself, a helpless victim, whose strength had been drained from the loss of blood. Gathering momentum to deliver the deadly blow, Gizurr lept up so high that the sky could be seen between his legs. The gratuitous ferocity of the blow was a measure of his hatred as was his callousness in allowing the corpse to be mutilated. Snorri was at this time in Norway. After his return he unaccountably neglected to guard himself against Gizurr. Ultimately Snorri proved to be unprepared for Gizurr's attack on his life.

We can only attempt to seek the answer to Snorri's ineffectual alliances and moves against Sturla. His signal restraint was remarkable especially after Órækja's mutilation and Sturla's occupation of Reykjaholt, where Snorri had spent the most glorious part of his life. *The Saga of the Icelanders* provides a partial answer. Snorri's brother Sighvatr pointed out to his son Sturla that despite Sturla's wrongful seizure of Snorri's possessions, Sturla's trouble would emanate from foes other than Snorri. Sighvatr, it seems, recognized Snorri's inner recoil from inflicting physical injury on his kinsmen. Yet Snorri's lack of spirit might also have been caused by a feeling of disappointment and despondency. Órækja, his only surviving son, lacked the essential qualities of a chieftain. He was an impulsive man flawed by the lack of foresight. Even before his mutilation, he was without the support of the peasantry, imprudently displayed coolness toward Sturla, and revealed his want of resources in Sturla's presence. Sturla explained before the mutilation of Órækja: "It doesn't seem advisable for him to live so near with such slight means while I wallow in Snorri's wealth" (ch. 15, p. 299). The consequences of Snorri's inability to check Sturla were grave: Snorri would not recapture the impetus to sustain his position as Iceland's most powerful chieftain.

Little is recorded about Snorri's second sojourn to Norway (1237–39) except that he was with his friend Jarl Skúli or with

Skúli's son. Jarl Skúli was now an enemy of the king and
Snorri's stay with Skúli accelerated his fate. In the two years he
spent in Norway, he did not seek out the king. When he sailed
to Iceland, he did so in open defiance of the king's ban. Rumors
also circulated that Skúli, in a secret ceremony, had made Snorri
his jarl. The rumor was serious, since Skúli was planning at this
period an ill-fated revolt against the king. Snorri's acceptance
of the jarl's title, a charge never proven, would signify that he
had been privy to Skúli's plans. Upon Snorri's return Gizurr
seized upon the king's equivocal order to have Snorri slain.
Snorri's death had advanced Gizurr's political goal to attain control over Iceland.

For Snorri's development as a writer his close ties to the
Norwegian court were fruitful. His knowledge of life at court
contributed to his insight into the glory and arrogance of kingship. For his own life and the independence of his country his
association proved fateful. His death was justified by the fact
that the king had judged him a traitor. Ever since he had been
appointed a baron, the first Icelander to be honored with the
title, he had been legally subordinate to the king. The possibility that Snorri may have yielded to the king the titles of two
of his land holdings in exchange for the honor may have also
affected his standing. The evidence is a terse statement in the
Annals of the Men from Oddi: "He [Snorri] was the first to cede
property to the king, namely Bersastaðir and Eyvindarstaðir."
After Snorri's death the king claimed these farms as well as
other land owned by Snorri on the grounds that Snorri had
committed treason.[23]

The king thus had a foothold in Iceland. This, together with
Gizurr's readiness to champion the king's cause, helped the king
some twenty years after Snorri's death to subjugate Iceland to
the Norwegian crown (1264). Ironically, an Icelandic chieftain
in *Heimskringla* observes in one of the most vivid scenes of
the work that it would be unwise to cede to the Norwegian king
even the most barren skerry. Yet Snorri, it seems, was the first
to compromise the independence of the island by granting the
king a claim to parcels of his land.

An unequivocal verdict on Snorri's life is difficult to arrive
at. For many years he projected himself as a chieftain who was

not to be trifled with. He loved splendor and displayed it with pride even during a winter when he lost a substantial portion of his livestock. His farm at Reykjaholt was a center of worldliness and the hub of his literary activity. Sturla Sighvatsson came there expressly to copy Snorri's sagas. Styrmir the Learned, who is credited with a lost version of the *Saga of Óláfr the Saint*, was a trusted member of Snorri's household. Hallbera, Snorri's daughter, only agreed to live with her first husband when he joined her at Reykjaholt. Yet Sturla the writer judges Snorri harshly, though objectively. Snorri had qualities indispensable for achieving dominance in Iceland's political life: energy, love of power, astuteness, and the ability to amass property. These qualities, as Sturla saw it, were offset by indecision at critical moments, lack of courage, and a miserliness which discouraged loyalty and furthered disaffection. In particular Sturla singles out Snorri's avarice as his controlling passion. By reporting a prophecy of his father Þórðr on Snorri's fate, Sturla attributes Snorri's death explicitly to his greed. Þórðr said that he feared "Snorri's wealth" might lead to Snorri's death, to his destruction either by water or by men (ch. 53, p. 200). Snorri's greed did contribute to his slaying. His stepsons joined Gizurr. One even participated in the follow-up expedition to the raid in which Snorri was killed. Interestingly, both possibilities in Þórðr's prophecy were realized. Snorri found his death by the sword, in part because of a royal letter from across the seas.

Nevertheless, we can infer from sparse comments that Snorri was a person of warmth and feeling. He felt intense grief at the death of his second wife and at the slaying of his brother Sighvatr. He was susceptible to the charm of women, to their beauty, wit, and elegance. Yet in his relations to his children we seldom sense an unreserved, unselfish love. Indeed his refusal to give his son Jón the marriage portion Jón desired was the indirect cause of Jón's death, for Jón in turn insisted on sailing to Norway where he was slain. The unhappy state of mind manifest in Snorri's children, is perhaps attributable to a lack of fatherly concern. We hear of Jón's drunkenness and uncontrollable temper, of Hallbera's joyless marriages, and of Ingibjörg's inability to live harmoniously with a husband who in later marriages demonstrated deep marital affection. Also Órækja's marriage was brief, for after his mutilation his wife left him. More importantly, however, we never see Snorri as a father giving good counsel and acting in concert with his children to further their goals. This absence of any incident revealing deep paternal solicitude seems part of a deliberate literary design to contrast Snorri's fatherhood to Sighvatr's. Sighvatr supports his son Sturla, warns him in a caustic game of role-casting of the pride that cometh before the fall, and joins him in the battle in which both father and son were to die. Indeed, Snorri's inability to instill loyalty that endures to death can be appreciated more fully by contrasting Sighvatr's death scene to Snorri's. Sighvatr was protected by a retainer shielding the exhausted old man. Even after Sighvatr had been wounded to death a companion, wishing to halt the mutilation of Sighvatr's corpse, covered Sighvatr's body with his own and was slain. Snorri, however, was given away by a houseguest fearing for his life and limbs.

During these twenty-one years of political intrigue, social accomplishment, and personal disappointment, we hear little of Snorri's literary activities. There are only two references to Snorri's literary interests, and these statements consist only of a handful of words. Sturla, the writer, tells us that his cousin Sturla Sighvatsson went to Snorri's farm to copy the sagabooks Snorri had composed. We also learn that Snorri's booth on the Althing was called Valhalla, named after the abode of Óðinn, the god of poetry and war. This constitutes our sole knowledge of Snorri's life as a writer. Only one bit of information supplements our meager knowledge of Snorri's interest in historic objects. Snorri had journeyed to Sweden during his first stay in Norway to seek out Frú Kristín, formerly the widow of Jarl Hákon galinn and now the wife of the lawspeaker Áskell. She gave him the battle flag which the Swedish king Eiríkr Knútsson had used during the battle of Gestilsreini (1210), in which he had felled King Sörkvir. Biographical information yields, hence, little knowledge about Snorri the writer. Only his works disclose the essence of his thoughts and the expansive range of his interests, manifest his mastery over and his development of saga style, and exemplify his scholarly and literary approach to the writing of Norwegian history.

CHAPTER 2

Snorri's Literary Heritage

I *The Development from Oral to Written Literature*

SNORRI wrote the *Edda* and *Heimskringla* approximately one hundred years after Old Norse works, all utilitarian in character, had first been committed to writing. Within the span of a mere century Iceland had turned from a society in which oral literature was cultivated exclusively to a society which was highly literate.[1] The stage of the transition from oral literature to a body of literature preserved by writing rather than by memory was not disruptive. Writing came into use for pragmatic reasons. Human memory, even at its best, was less retentive and reliable than parchment manuscripts. In a society which prided itself on its self-government by law, on its recent conversion to Christianity, and on the kinship of its leading families to prominent settlers from Norway, writing became a means to preserve and transmit its body of law, Christian values and legends, genealogies, and historical lore.[2]

During the fifty years following Iceland's first use of writing as a tool to preserve and instruct crucial matters of daily life, all writings had a learned, didactic, or pragmatic character. The Church had a vital interest in written documents. They spread the knowledge of ecclesiastical laws and encouraged its observance, while charters recorded church property and discouraged infringement of property rights. Just as the Church had been instrumental in the introduction of writing, church leaders continued to encourage the use of writing even for matters not totally of an ecclesiastical nature. Indeed the existence of written ecclesiastical laws may well have influenced the writing of secular law. Church leaders, we surmise, convinced the leading chieftains, who were often their kinsmen, of the practical advantages

35

of a body of secular law preserved and transmitted by writing.

The intellectual and kinship associations between the Icelandic ecclesiastical leaders and chieftains account also for the adoption of Icelandic as the preferred medium of writing. As the century wore on, Latin fell more and more into disuse, so much so in fact that historical works or pseudohistorical works written in Latin were either lost because of disinterest or survived only in Icelandic translations or, to be more precise, Icelandic adaptations. In addition there were in Iceland oral poems of dramatic power and passages of lyrical beauty. Probably also oral sagas were told which employed narrative techniques characteristic of the classical sagas of the thirteenth century. This love of Icelandic writers and poets for their own language was of utmost importance for the development of Snorri. The use of the vernacular in historical works, the sagas of the Norwegian missionary kings, Óláfr Tryggvason and Óláfr Haraldsson, and oral sagas nurtured in Snorri a saga style that was both dependent on existing narrative forms and critical of the literary flaws in historical and pseudohistorical hagiographic works: their discursiveness, lack of internal structure, and particularly the improbable constellation of events found occasionally in the sagas on the missionary kings. Snorri, schooled in the art of oral saga telling, developed a written style that was terse, succinct, and dramatic. Concentrating on the memorable, Snorri subordinated all details of a dramatic episode to one end: the powerful revelation of character and conduct. This technique of visualization was an essential part of oral saga telling, a technique which Snorri exploited fully in his vivid recreation of the mythological and historical past. Snorri's art is in essence based on the narrative devices of oral literature, though he has honed his style and tightened the presentation of his material by applying and furthering the critical standards of a learned community.

The standards Snorri admired and emulated were the critical standards applied to historic truth in Icelandic historical literature. Within one hundred and fifty years after the acceptance of Christianity the first serious historical works were being written. Interest in history, in historical events, in the ancestry of prominent historical figures and their character, was part of Icelandic cultural tradition. This historic interest was also nurtured by the Church, by the education of several outstanding Icelanders in ecclesiastical schools in Germany, France, and England, and by the awareness of ecclesiastical leaders that historic works, written accounts of the deeds of the past, had been cultivated for centuries in the non-Scandinavian world.[3] The interest derived from both native and ecclesiastical traditions came to coalesce because the leaders of the Church and secular chieftains were closely related by blood and shared the native cultural heritage as well as some common secular and ecclesiastical concerns. Chieftains, the administrators of the things, were up to 1190 the owners of churches and church property. They were therefore intimately involved in ecclesiastical administration and legal reforms.

II *Literary Models and Precursors*

The first historians were closely associated with the Church. Men who devoted their lives to the Church or to monastic life were responsible initially for the writing of sagas. Monks wrote the first sagas on the missionary king Óláfr Tryggvason, and ecclesiastical thinking and feeling permeated the first versions of the saga on Óláfr the Saint. The *Sagas of the Bishops* were written under the auspices of the Church, and Karl Jónsson, an abbot, wrote the first part of the *Saga of King Sverrir* according to the king's own account of his adventurous and battle-filled life.

Sæmundr Sigfússon (1056–1133), the first historian of the literary age, was a deacon educated in France and the builder and therefore owner of a renowned church on his family estate. He was commemorated as the first who put into writing facts relating to the lives of the Norwegian kings. His history, however, was lost presumably because of the language and character of the work. Sæmundr wrote in Latin and his work, we assume, consisted of little more than dry notices on events during the reign of the Norwegian kings, events which he linked to prominent dates in European history. Snorri fails to mention Sæmundr as one of his models, probably because Sæmundr's work went counter to Snorri's conception of history as a recreation of the past which by its lifelike texture enabled man to know and to cope with the present.

The historian whom Snorri admired deeply was Ari Þorgilsson (1067/68–1148). Only one slim work of Ari has survived, *The Book of the Icelanders* (written between 1122 and 1133). Yet this book, which consists of a mere ten pages or so of printed text, reveals those qualities of mind and craftsmanship which Snorri praised unreservedly in the prologue to *Heimskringla*. Ari, Snorri said, held historic truth in high regard, had a well-informed and trained mind, and had acquired his knowledge of history from mentors with a reputation for historical truthfulness and interest, men who had witnessed some of the signal events of their era, and who had lived to an advanced age. Ari's historic sense was hence based on his superior mental endowment and training as well as on the critical sense, acuity of memory, and an intense interest in contemporary events which distinguished his informants. Snorri does not mention Ari's style. Indeed a portion of Ari's surviving work is merely factual and is devoid of the suspense and imaginative verve which typify the best of saga writing. Nevertheless he described the scene closest to him intellectually and emotionally, the acceptance of Christianity at the Althing, with the vigor and descriptive power of a major saga writer.

Ari had been ordained a priest and ecclesiastical influence pervaded his life and even determined the structure and contents of *The Book of the Icelanders*. Ari's grandfather had died while returning from a pilgrimage to Rome and Ari himself had been educated by Teitr (d. 1110), the son of Bishop Ísleifr and the brother of Bishop Gizurr. Both Teitr's father and brother had been trained at Hereford, Westphalia, and their European education in all probability influenced Teitr's teaching and therefore Ari's schooling. In later life Ari wrote with the support, encouragement, and criticism of the bishops Þorlákr and Ketill. Ari submitted the first version of *The Book of the Icelanders* (a version that has been lost) to both bishops and to Sæmundr Sigfússon and revised it according to their wishes and the new information he had acquired. The book we know is the revised edition.

The circumstances relating to the origin of the surviving *Book of the Icelanders* are interesting in that they demonstrate that the two bishops of Iceland had commissioned a book of the Icelanders, a work which also contained matters of a purely secular nature. Also noteworthy is the fact that Ari, despite his priesthood and close associations with the two Icelandic prelates, received his most trustworthy information of the past from unlettered but knowledgeable historians who were exactingly trained in the memorization of signal events of their times.

There was not only an interest in past history but also a lively concern to preserve accurately contemporary affairs. Abbot Karl Jónsson composed part of the *Saga of King Sverrir* according to the king's testimony and the abbot's own sense of objectivity and dedication to historic accuracy. An earlier work, *Hryggjarstykki* (1170), by Eiríkr Oddson, though no longer extant, treated, as we know from Snorri and from another source, the lives of Norwegian kings during part of the twelfth century, probably from 1130–1161. Like Ari, Eiríkr relied on oral informants, some of whom Snorri identified as officials or courtiers of the Norwegian kings. One was present at the torture-slaying of King Sigurðr slembidjákn (d. 1139), a scene described by Eiríkr and copied by Snorri. Both Ari and Eiríkr are described similarly in medieval sources, as wise men with critical judgment. Eiríkr, however, surpasses Ari in verbal command and skill in narrative structure. Sigurður Nordal ascribes the vividness of Eiríkr's style and the richness of detail to the emotional impact of contemporary affairs; G. Turville-Petre, conversely, believes that there was a progressive improvement of style throughout the century and that Eiríkr's work exemplifies this stylistic development.[4]

G. Turville-Petre also posits a pervasive influence of ecclesiastical learning on the development of saga style: "Foreign learning and foreign letters helped . . . to preserve ancient memories and to express traditional thoughts" (p. 109). This premise seems, however, overstated in other parts of his work. To be sure, the cathedral schools at Skálaholt and Hólar and the monastery of Þingeyrar were important centers for the writing of the *Bishop Sagas,* the early versions of the sagas of Óláfr Tryggvason by Oddr Snorrason and Gunnlaugr Leifsson, homiletic literature, translations from popular medieval ecclesiastical writings, and the composition of the *Saga of King Sverrir*. Indubitably the writing of hagiographic literature had influenced the writing

of sagas, for both the lives of saints and the sagas concentrated
on the heroism of the main characters. Saga writers probably
also adopted from ecclesiastical models the mechanics of
dividing narrative material into chapters. The essential framework, the narrative unit, however, existed in oral saga telling. A
saga had to be told in units. As sagas were recited on consecutive
evenings saga tellers had to allow for the shortness of the eve-
ning hours and the brevity of the listeners' attention span.[5]

Whether the influence of ecclesiastical writings on saga literature was as great as G. Turville-Petre assumes, is therefore at
best a moot question. The chronology of the *Bishop Sagas* and
the best of the earliest *Kings' Sagas* suggest that the two
genres were developing concurrently. The *Saga of Bishop Jón*
was written after 1201; *Hungrvaka* and *Þorláks saga* were
written between 1195 and 1211; and the *Saga of Páll the Bishop*
probably after 1211. Also the *Saga of King Sverrir* and the
Saga of the Orkney Jarls were being composed at that time. These
were the sagas Snorri must have heard or had read when he was
young and had begun to form his own literary style.[6] The ecclesiastical sagas on the bishops and the missionary kings, while
an inspiration, had a less direct effect on his style than native
tradition. Native tradition was marked by the strong historic
sense of saga writers whose great interest in history discouraged
the uncritical use of miracles and tales of magic which typify
hagiographic literature.

When Snorri started to compose the first and central part of
Heimskringla, the *Saga of Óláfr the Saint,* there was not a
single work which could serve him as a model for the rigorous
standards of literary and historical excellence that he would
set for himself. The sagas on the two missionary kings, Óláfr
Tryggvason and Óláfr the Saint, were hagiographic in matter,
origin, and expression.[7] Snorri, conversely, saw Óláfr the Saint
as a chieftain who primarily sought power and who had used
Christianity as a weapon to fulfill his ambition. For Snorri,
Óláfr became a saint only in defeat. By the irony of fate, in
Christian terms by predestination, Óláfr exchanged in his last
battle his earthly kingdom for the governance of a spiritual
realm: Óláfr came to be recognized as Norway's eternal king.
For these reasons the miracles in *Heimskringla* take place only

during the final period of Óláfr's life, his exile in Russia, and after his death on the battlefield.

This is essentially a rational view of Óláfr, a view supported and strengthened by Snorri's reflection on the personality and acts of his friend the Icelandic bishop Guðmundr (1203–1237), who after his death was also declared a saint. Guðmundr, like Óláfr, had ruthlessly employed religion as a weapon to expand his power and thereby the power of the medieval Icelandic church. Throughout Snorri's work there is the awareness that despite the passing of time, human conduct and motivation remain alike.

Snorri was committed to historical truth, which for Snorri was vouched for by the works of Ari Þorgilsson and by skaldic poems which were contemporaneous to the events described or which were composed shortly thereafter. Snorri realized that historic truth was ascertainable from the time of Óláfr Tryggvason's brief reign to his own period (995 to ca. 1220), for there were reliable accounts of events even during the early part of the time span. For the period of Óláfr Tryggvason's reign, there was trustworthy testimony transmitted by a contemporary of Óláfr Tryggvason. This oral historian had also been an eyewitness to signal events at the beginning of Óláfr's reign and had imparted his knowledge to Ari's most trusted informant. For the period preceding Óláfr Tryggvason's reign there were some skaldic poems as there were for succeeding periods as well as tales. These tales, though not historic in matter, illustrated a verity or disclosed personality traits traditionally ascribed to well-known historic figures. The tales provided insight into historic processes and the character of leaders, information therefore not easily transmitted by unadorned statements, factual knowledge, or the eulogistic phraseology of the skalds.

Though the scope of Snorri's history was far more comprehensive than that of any other surviving history of the Norwegian kings, several synoptic histories were written during 1190–1220. Two of these works, *Ágrip* and *Fagrskinna*, were written in Norway. Both were modest in scale and artistic achievement. Of these Snorri knew *Ágrip*. He had admired the author's telling of a love tale so much that he copied it almost

verbatim in his version of the *Saga of Haraldr the Fairhaired.*[8]
Snorri may have consulted *Fagrskinna,* the work of a contemporary and compatriot, who also cited numerous skaldic
verses to buttress his account of the history of the Norwegian
kings. Noteworthy is the circumstance that *Fagrskinna* was
written for the Norwegian king, for the writing of *Heimskringla*
was probably also inspired by the interest of the Norwegian
regent and the young king. The patronage of the Norwegian
court did much to stimulate the writing of history. The *Sagas
of Kings* are at their best informative, instructive, and literarily
sophisticated, as desired by an aristocratic, discriminating
audience.

Snorri also knew a third synoptic history in its original
form, a collection of sagas preserved in a manuscript called
Morkinskinna, "Rotten Skin." The original manuscript, now lost,
is dated around 1200. It is unknown whether or not *Morkinskinna*
is a reliable copy of the original manuscript. What is striking
about the style of the surviving version of *Morkinskinna* is the
author's delight in storytelling. His skill in creating vivid
scenes equals that found in the *Family Sagas.* What is lacking
in *Morkinskinna* is structure, a framework tight enough to lend
cohesiveness to the stories linked tangentially to Norway's
rulers. In *Heimskringla* Snorri demonstrated his mastery over
both form and expression. His skill in interweaving the many
strands of his narrative and in composing scenes that were both
pithy and dramatic was unmatched at his time. None of the
synoptics equals *Heimskringla* in the scope of its historic vision,
its power of characterization, and verbal and structural command. Snorri was indisputably the master of saga writing, yet he
was only one writer during a time of thriving literary activity.
Perhaps only the vagaries of transmission or the priority that
early writers gave to the sagas on Norwegian kings and Icelandic
bishops are responsible for the fact that the very best of the
Family Sagas were generally committed to writing only after
Snorri's death.

CHAPTER 3

The Prose Edda

I *Introduction*

S NORRI'S best-known and most popular work is probably the
Prose Edda.[1] With the exception of some skaldic poems it is
also the earliest work Snorri composed. Its history of origin
is interesting. Snorri first conceived and executed a part of
the work that today is read only by specialists, a long poem and
metrical commentary named *Háttatal, "Enumeration of Poetical
Meters."* In modern editions and in the manuscripts this part is
the third and last section of the work, a position which indicates
that the composition lacks intrinsic interest. In composing the
poem Snorri had two objectives in mind. First the poem eulogized
the Norwegian regent Jarl Skúli and the child-king Hákon
Hákonarson, whom Snorri had sought out at the Norwegian
court. Secondly, the poem illustrated the many forms of versification that were and could be used in skaldic art. The conception
of the poem as a poetic encomium and compedium of versification suggests that Snorri from the very beginning conceived
himself as a skald and educator.

This role as educator led Snorri to the expansion of the work.
Snorri realized that in his era, when knowledge of the heathen
period and its poetic tradition was no longer commonplace, the
complexity of skaldic metaphoric language had to be explained.
This he did in *Skáldskaparmál, "Poetic Diction,"* the second part
of the *Prose Edda*. In *Skáldskaparmál* Snorri explained the
myths and heroic legends on which kennings[2] were based.
Kennings are the distinctive feature of skaldic poetic language.
Only a firm knowledge of that tradition would ensure the
existence of an art of poetry that after the conversion had
undergone a checkered development and which in Snorri's
time was losing vitality.

In *Skáldskaparmál* Snorri had modified a frame used in the Eddic poem "Vafþrúðnismál," a wisdom poem, in which Óðinn and the giant Vafþrúðnir competed with each other in exhibiting their knowledge of the mythic world. The prize to be won was, sardonically, the loser's head. In *Skáldskaparmál*, the situation has lost its sting. The frame's setting is a social occasion in which the giant Ægir, host of the gods, asks Bragi, the god of poetry, to explain kennings and to tell the stories which led to the poetic genesis of the kennings. The innocuous narrative situation, the inability to form a cohesive narrative with this type of frame, and perhaps a sense of boredom with a structure that stipulated the mere enumeration of parcels of knowledge, inspired the conception of *Gylfaginning*, "*The Delusion of Gylfi.*"

Gylfaginning is also a compendium structured in question-and-answer form. Yet the frame and the main body of the work are interwoven. Gylfi, the pagan king of Sweden, sets out to interrogate the Æsir on the source of their power. The Æsir, represented by three mysterious figures in high seats placed one above the other, recount the mythic course of the world, the names and functions of the deities, and some of the major myths. Gylfi accepts their accounts and because he had asked the right questions and had internalized the answers, he does not lose his head, but finds himself at the close of the session in a field, ready to convert his people to believe in and worship the Æsir. The frame accordingly explains why the Scandinavian world came to venerate the Æsir. The Æsir deluded Gylfi and ensnared him into a false belief because he, like all pagans, lacked the spiritual illumination which can only be conferred by God.

II   Gylfaginning, "The Delusion of Gylfi"

The reputation of the *Prose Edda* rests principally upon *Gylfaginning*,[3] the only section of the tripartite work to present Northern mythology as an autonomous cycle, from the birth and creation of the universe to the destruction of the cosmos and its rebirth. The myths Snorri tells about the gods of the Viking Age are masterpieces in the art of storytelling and are likewise an invaluable source of Scandinavian mythology. In contrast to

the Eddic poems, which are often cryptic and difficult to understand for those untrained in Northern mythology, the tales
convey a sense of intimacy with the world of the gods. After
reading *Gylfaginning*, we, like Gylfi, understand how the world
was created. We recognize the precariousness of existence, know
the character of the deities, and appreciate the timelessness of
their functions. In narrating the course of the world in its glory,
precariousness, and collapse, Snorri elicits in us the empathic
certainty that this is how the world was created, this is what
the gods did, and this is how the world will come to an end.

The name *Gylfaginning, "The Delusion of Gylfi,"* is puzzling
until we recognize that the term has an important religious
function and that the structure of the narrative situation would
be familiar to any medieval reader or listener. The name is
derived from the narrative situation. Gylfi, king of Sweden, is
tricked into accepting the Æsir as gods. His factual and spiritual
delusion and his role as missionary king explain why many
generations of illustrious and intelligent men blindly believed
in the power of pagan divinities and were oblivious to the
existence of God. The structure of the narrative situation is
typically medieval. Gylfi asks questions of knowledge. He
receives answers from three manifestations of Óðinn, all of whom
are by implication omniscient. This is the characteristically
medieval way to impart book knowledge. The student who is
ignorant but eager to learn is regarded as a vessel for the
reception of facts. In Old Norse pagan poetry the situation is
somewhat different. Two equally knowledgeable mythical personages confront each other in a competition to establish their
intellectual superiority in the command over mythical knowledge.
In not a single poem, even not in poems in which the questioner
seeks knowledge through necromancy, is the questioner ignorant
of the main facts and events of the mythological past and present.
This change in the native narrative tradition, Gylfi's appearance
as an ignorant rather than a knowledgeable questioner, has an
important function. His ignorance lends plausibility to the
supposition that a state of spiritual ignorance caused the worship
of the Æsir.

Gylfaginning seems to have an abrupt and digressive beginning.
The introduction is an etiological tale set in the land of Gylfi,

King of Sweden. King Gylfi promised a vagabond woman a
piece of plowland to reward her for some entertainment. The
woman who bears the telling name Gefjon, "the Giver," and
who belongs to the divine family of the Æsir, plowed off a
huge piece of land with the help of four oxen, her giant sons,
and had the land mass dragged into the sea. This was the birth
of the island of Zealand.

At first reading, this tale has little to do with the body of
Snorri's mythological narrative about the birth of the universe,
its governance, and its destruction. Even Gefjon is only one of
the minor deities in the mythological account. Yet in a mythical
sense the tale has an illuminative function. The tale explains
Gylfi's desire to fathom the source of the Æsir's power and also
initiates and demonstrates from the very beginning the successful
delusion of Gylfi. Gylfi had thought that he was bestowing on a
vagabond woman a land gift of little account. In fact he gave
a substantial land mass to one of the Æsir. The narrative itself,
the formation of Zealand, is for Snorri only of peripheral importance. The mythical implications of the tale are significant.
The tale explains why Gylfi sought to establish the source of the
Æsir's power and simultaneously testifies to Gylfi's psychological
readiness to accept the Æsir as gods. The delusion of Gylfi begins
in the etiological tale.

The theme of delusion and self-deception reoccurs in the
account of Gylfi's visit to Ásgarðr, the home of the gods, and
becomes the main theme of Gylfi's confrontation with and dis-
missal by the Æsir. Gylfi intends to be unknown. He changes
himself into an old man. In contrast to Gylfi's inability to recognize Gefjon, the Æsir are fully aware of Gylfi's disguise and
implicitly know the reason for his visit.

Gylfi's assumed name, Gangleri, "the Wayworn," serves to
underscore Gylfi's blindness, since Gangleri is ironically also a
name for Óðinn. The assumption of an Óðinn-name points to
Gylfi's presumptuousness in attempting to outwit the gods at
their own game. Óðinn is wise and cunning. He has fore-
knowledge, or can gain it by magic. Gylfi, though he pretends
to be Gangleri, cannot recognize the delusion wrought by magic.
Also, on a secular level, the name Gangleri evokes an ironic
smile. The name refers to a man who by his constant travels

had acquired breadth and depth of knowledge. Gangleri-Gylfi, however, is shown up as a man who lacks insight into the hidden. The use of the name Gangleri therefore supports the function of the introduction: to demonstrate that Gangleri, who like all pagans lacks divine illumination, cannot resist the persuasiveness of the mythic accounts which ascribe divinity to the Æsir.

The opening scenes introduce Gylfi as a promising acolyte. His mind being that of a heathen can be manipulated. The symbols of power with which the gods usher him into their presence are frightening. Gylfi perceives virtuoso sword juggling, an immense hall thatched with golden shields, grim entertainment, and uncanny fighting in the numerous sections of the giant hall. This is a display of power unknown to Gylfi, a power he feels is threatening. Indeed, the power Gylfi recognizes is intended to be menacing. A door through which Gylfi steps closes behind his heels and for his presumptuous inquiry into the Æsir's might, the three hosts all bearing bynames of Óðinn ("the High-one," "Just-as-High," and "the Third") threaten him with the loss of his head, if he proves to be less wise than they are.

The display of power and the enactments of martial games initiate Gylfi into the mythical domain of Óðinn, the god of war and presumptive creator and governor of the world. The mise-en-scène of Óðinn's power foreshadows that Gylfi will ultimately accept Óðinn as the paternal head of the pantheon and that we, with Gylfi's mediation, will accept this too. We come to believe that the supreme power has always been vested in Óðinn and that he with the aid of his co-divinities governs the earth and the sky. Accordingly, we tend to forget that in *Gylfaginning* the agrarian gods, Þórr and Freyr, occupy undeservedly subaltern positions. The delusion of Gylfi has thus also affected our minds. Also we are unable to question the persuasive truth of the mythological account.

Despite the intimidation and occasional mocking reproof, Gylfi deports himself with dignity. His questioning is direct and to the point. Gylfi wants to know the name of the most powerful god and his credentials. Who is the highest of the gods, where is he, what can he do, and which works testify to his greatness? The answers are as clearcut as the questions. Gylfi hears the twelve names of Óðinn, which confirm the god's extensive might.

This god is the creator and governor of the world and the maker of man. Óðinn's credentials are established by his comprehensive account of a world unborn, of the forces existing in chaos and the birth of life in the form of both monstrous giants and the ancestor of the Æsir. Quotations from Eddic poems vouch for the truthfulness of the account. In these poems, purported to be from the mythological past, giants, enemies of Óðinn, recite the facts of creation and the course of the mythological world or accept facts and events as Óðinn recapitulates them. The authoritative and seemingly honest recital of these divine credentials turns Gylfi from an unbeliever into a willing disciple and furtherer of the Æsir's cult.

Snorri was concerned, as any medieval man would be, with the problem of evil. What caused evil and what were the manifestations of evil? The answers Snorri found in Old Norse mythology were different from the answers given in the Bible. Man's disobedience toward God the Creator, man's disregard of God's commands are themes which have no counterpart in Old Norse mythology and in the *Prose Edda*. Evil is originally an impersonal force which comes into existence with the creation of life itself, or to be more exact, evil or the forces of destruction are present prior to the creation of life. "At first there was this world in the South which is called Múspell: It is bright and hot; this world is burning and in flames. It is perilous to those who are strangers and do not have their homes there" (ch. 4, p. 11).[4] In the North there are poisonous rivers the waters of which hardened to ice. Paradoxically, these forces which by their very nature are hostile to life, create life. Where the hot air and ice met, life was formed in the shape of Ymir, an enormous bisexual giant, who in his sleep created two sons and a daughter. A primordial cow emerged from the ice. The cow fed Ymir with four rivers of milk. Thus life was created and sustained.

Despite the existence of the forces of destruction, life engendered life in multiple forms to counterbalance the ravages of death and to ensure the development of the universe. The cow which fed Ymir uncovered a being in the shape of a man from beneath the ice. His descendants, Óðinn, Vili, and Vé, were the primordial gods of the North. They would create the world by killing Ymir and would then impose social order.

Evil has no moral implications in the greater part of *Gylfa-ginning*. The killing of Ymir provided the material essential for the formation of the universe. Ymir's body formed the earth, his blood the sea, rivers, and lakes, the skull the sky, his bones the mountains, and his brains the clouds. His destruction and the subsequent creation of the world from his body seem hence ordained by a law of nature. Death, even violent death, is the basis for a rebirth of life and the creation of a higher order.

Óðinn and his two alter egos express their pride in their creation. There is only a tinge of apprehension in their early admission that, although most giants drowned in the blood of Ymir, one escaped with his wife by climbing on his *lúðr*, or "coffin." This giant was the father of all subsequent giants, giants intent on destroying the universe and the order created by Óðinn, Vili, and Vé. The forces of destruction were hence still part of the universe. They were no longer embodied in simple, elementary forces of nature, but in giants, beings whose powers rivaled those of the gods except in one aspect. Giants in *Gylfaginning* were inimical to social order.

Coexisting with the universe were hence its enemies, giants deprived of their right to preeminence and anxious to regain it. This the gods took into account as they ordered the created world. In defining and localizing the realms of the world they settled the giants on the edge of the earth, on the outermost reaches of land girded by the sea. This containment of the giants not only symbolizes their hostility toward the divine universe but also expresses the gods' policy toward their rivals to power. Giants cannot be defeated. They can only be confined up to the preordained time of *Ragnarök*, "the doom of the gods," when the universe will be destroyed and a higher order will be born.

Contrary to the sequence in "Völuspá," the poem which was one of Snorri's most important sources, Snorri ascribes the creation of man to an early phase in the making of the universe. The gods create man before they establish the sequence of day and night. In this brief myth consisting of only six printed lines Snorri summarizes the creative faculties of the gods. They give life to inert matter, to two unshapen, lifeless, wooden blocks. They bestow breath, senses, form, intellect, and emotions and they present a social order symbolized by the clothes and names given to primeval man and woman. It is as if Snorri wished to emphasize in this. myth what was not readily apparent in the myth on the creation of the world, namely that the gods do not only form and order matter, but also endow matter with life.

The process of creation is protracted and creation is finite. While the gods are establishing the basic functions of the earth, the alternation of day and night, Snorri points to the fragility of their work by providing two consecutive illustrations of the world's impermanence. He refers to the sun's fright of her pursuer, the wolf who will swallow her at Ragnarök. The sun's terror, the gods confirm, is well founded. They thus acknowledge that their creation is subject to the cycle of life and death. Yet they also confirm by continuing their account of creation that the temporality of their achievement does not flaw the glory of their accomplishments. Despite the ultimate destruction facing their universe, the gods still establish their halls, create the dwarves, fashion tools, work metal, stone, and wood, and arrange for the workings of fate. This will to persist, to continue their work and to defend creation despite the sure knowledge of defeat is palpable in the myth on Bifrǫst, the mythic bridge which leads from the earth to Ásgarðr, the realm of the gods. Gangleri is amazed that the gods would build a bridge that was too weak to withstand the assault of the giants at Ragnarök. The reply to Gangleri is an unequivocal rebuttal of the charge that the gods were lax in constructing the bridge: "The gods do not deserve censure because of this structure. Bifrǫst is a good bridge, but in this world there is nothing which will hold once Múspell's sons begin their attack (ch. 6, pp. 18-20).

The gods' admission that their creation is temporal and finite is based upon their recognition that in creating the world they have created instruments of destruction, giants who would not forget that the creation of the universe had threatened their existence. The gods refer openly to their giant adversaries' might in brief phrases on the coming of Ragnarök and in a description of a universe that from its inception is flawed. Yggdrasill, the cosmic tree, under which the gods hold judgment, suffers decay because of a mythic snake which gnaws at its roots and because of four deer which eat its branches. By commenting that Baldr's horse is burned on the pyre with the body of its master, the gods allude to the slaying of Baldr, the innocent god. The full account of the slaying of Baldr will precede the description of Ragnarök, for Baldr's death signals the imminent doom of the gods.

The first part of *Gylfaginning* is structured around two themes: 1) Óðinn, the primordial creator, is beyond the shadow of a doubt the chief deity; 2) The inevitability of Ragnarök is felt as an ever-present force in all of creation. These two themes are interwoven only sporadically in the second section which deals with the deities' attributes and power. The theme of Óðinn's predominance is reiterated once at the beginning of the second section (ch. 11, p. 27). He is the highest and oldest among the Æsir and governs all things. All other gods are his sons, or, as Snorri describes the relationship euphemistically, they all accord him the respect given a father by his sons. With this declaration Snorri falsifies religious history and misrepresents to a certain degree the mythic knowledge he had acquired. Only an allusion to the cult war between the Æsir and the Vanir, the Norse fertility gods, indicates that Óðinn's reign had ever been challenged or that Óðinn was not the most venerated god in the North. Njörðr, the chief god of the Vanir, is introduced not as one of the Vanir, but as the third *áss* (singular of Æsir). Freyr, Njörðr's son, is said to be the most famous deity among the Æsir and Freyja, his sister, the most honored among the *Ásynjar*, "the female deities of the Æsir." In the case of Njörðr, Snorri rectifies the record by stating that Njörðr was brought up among the Vanir and came to the Æsir as a hostage. Yet even this amplification is inconsequential. Interestingly, the theme of Óðinn's preeminence is pursued only tangentially, if at all, in the well-told myths of the second section, although in previous accounts Óðinn had been accorded the honor of being both the creator of the universe and the founder of social order.

After reaffirming the primacy of Óðinn, the other Norse deities are introduced. Snorri enumerates the gods, describes their mythic functions, and intersperses the recital of myths with a presentation of mythic facts and objects. These myths constitute the high point of Snorri's storytelling. They are tersely told tales without exegesis. They embody human experiences or appeal to human emotions. Accordingly, the mythic content of these tales has been secularized and becomes apparent only upon reflection. Solely the actors are divine.

The first tale, which relates the separation of Njörðr and Skaði, his bride, illustrates the secularization of a myth. The story illuminates wistfully the incompatibility of the marriage partners. From beginning to end the story concentrates on this facet of the marriage. Their innate inability to live together surfaces in the marriage conditions. Njörðr, a sea god, is to spend nine days in the wilderness of the mountains, Skaði's home, and Skaði is to stay the next nine days at the shore in Njörðr's domain. The first ten days break the marriage. Njörðr, upon his return to the shore, laments in a verse his distaste for the mountains. Skaði, in turn, complains that the screeching of the gulls destroys her sleep.

> Njörðr: Mountains I loathed
>
>   . . .
>   the howling of wolves
>   seemed ugly to me
>   compared with the hooping of swans.
> Skaði: I could not sleep
>   by the shore of the sea
>   for the sound of the mew
>   that awakened me,
>   the bird that flew
>   each dawn from the deep.[5]

The myth is short. Together with the verses it comprises only fourteen lines in the printed edition. Yet its brevity and the absence of censure lay bare a fundamental human problem, the hopelessness of a marriage with incompatible partners. Even the willingness to compromise on basic issues furthers solely the postponement of irreconcilable conflict, as rational arrangements are destroyed by emotion. Of course, the ease of divine divorce implicitly reflects the uncomplicated divorce procedures in pagan society. Incompatibility in marriage did not have to be endured. Even the gods practiced divorce.

The tale on Freyr's love for the giantess Gerðr is a falsified summary of the Eddic poem "Skírnismál." Snorri emphasizes the symptoms of a young man's lovesickness, a sickness so intense and sincere, that he pledges to his emissary his magic sword, the only sword which would have assured him victory in the battle with the giant Surtr at Ragnarök. Again the elements of danger are deemphasized in order to stress the mythic beauty of the giantess, a beauty so brilliant that the earth and sea reflected her radiance. The poem expresses the giantess's hostility toward Freyr and highlights the dire magic to be used, should she continue to refuse Freyr. Snorri conversely lingers exclusively on the young man's utter disregard of social conventions and on the social obstacles to the match. Characteristically the only citation from the poem is Freyr's confession of unrestrainable fervor when he hears that the giantess will meet him.

Even myths which exemplify the imminent imperilment of the universe are largely stripped of a sense of threat and endangerment. Both the myth on the binding of the Fenriswolf and the myth of the giant builder are adventurous tales rather than myths illustrating a cosmic struggle. The grim and foreboding aspects of the Fenriswolf myth have been deemphasized. They are used only to heighten suspense. The focus is on the emotions and deliberations of the mythic actors. The wolf allows himself to be fettered three times after the gods propose to the wolf successive trials of strength. The first time the chain is obviously weak. The second time the wolf realizes that even if the chain is stronger he also has grown and gained in strength. The third time, when the gods show him a fetter that is as thin as a cord of silk, his suspicions are aroused. He demands as a pledge of sincerity that one of the gods place his hand between his jaws. From this point on the interest shifts to the innate selfishness of the gods. They are dumbfounded and except for Týr are unprepared to sacrifice their right hand for the good of all. In simple but stark language Snorri highlights their callousness once more at the end of the myth. As the wolf writhes helplessly "all [the gods] laughed, except for Týr; he lost his hand" (ch. 21, p. 37). The demon had been bested momentarily. That is the important thing, while the loss of Týr's hand is inconsequential. Throughout the narrative the liveliness of the account takes precedence over the danger posed by the cosmic wolf. Snorri could not reconcile the theme of cosmic struggle with the adventurous tone of the story.

This lack of gravity in recounting myths in which the existence of the universe is threatened, is also palpable in the myth of the giant builder. The myth is a guileful and beguiling tale. Loki inveigles his co-divinities into allowing a giant to attempt the building of Ásgarðr, the fortress of the gods, within one season. The giant's reward is to be the sun, the moon, and Freyja. As soon as the gods realize that the giant will fulfill his part of the bargain, they force Loki to prevent the builder from completing the structure. Loki changes himself into a mare and prevents the giant's stallion from executing his nightly task. In Snorri's description this is a humorous episode which completely represses the sense of danger and apprehension which primitive man must have felt at the thought of the disappearance of the earth's fertility, the destruction of the summer season, and the extinction of day and night. This sense of danger is palpable in the Eddic poem "Völuspá, and is even more evident in the drastic solution to this impending disaster. In "Völuspá," stanza 26, Þórr breaks the gods' oaths to the giant builder and thus transgresses against the moral order set by the gods. In Snorri's account, the breaking of oaths is presented lightheartedly. Þórr, the god of brute strength, arrives. Ignoring the oaths he shatters the giant's skull into thousands of pieces. The episode has no major consequence for the course of the universe. Even the sequel makes light of the event. After nine months Loki bears an eight-legged horse, Sleipnir, the best of all horses, which becomes Óðinn's well-known steed. The episode which in "Völuspá"[6] is calamitous and foreshadows the destruction of the material and moral universe, is transformed by Snorri into a delightful tale of divine adventure.

Two myths on Þórr, his visit to Útgarðaloki and his hapless attempt to kill the Miðgarðssnake, belong to the most entertaining myths of *Gylfaginning*. They are somber reminders that the strongest of the gods is no match for the most powerful giants and that not even Þórr can avert by force the working of fate. Þórr will be impotent not once but twice during his adventures in giantland. The first myth opens with a story which intimates the powerlessness of Þórr in his ultimate endeavor to secure the universe from the onslaught of giants. Þórr, while staying at a farmer's house, slaughters his goats. He invites the farmer and his household to partake of the meat, but enjoins them to cast the bones on the skins of the goats. The next morning as Þórr resuscitates the goats by consecrating their skins with his hammer, he notices that one of the goats is lame. The farmer's son had split a thigh bone to extract the marrow. In atonement Þórr takes the boy as his servant. Despite the good ending the message of the episode is clear. One of Þórr's goats, animals intimately associated with Þórr's functions as a fertility god and as the god of thunder, is maimed. This is a portentous sign of Þórr's ultimate failure to ward off Ragnarök and, more immediately, is also an omen that his journey to giantland will be ill-starred. Because of the giants' superior control over magic and their physical strength, Þórr will succumb as he will at Ragnarök, although he will continue to slay giants of lesser stature.

From beginning to end the tale is an unrelieved putdown of Þórr. He is drawn into the giant's power by a magic darkness which envelops him and his companions. He seeks lodgings in a hall that turns out to be the giant Útgarðaloki's (alias Skrýmir) glove. He mistakes the giant's snoring for a continuous earthquake and agrees smallheartedly to accompany the giant on a journey. Although his hammer seems to sink into the giant's skull, he fails three times to kill the giant. Þórr's violence merely disrupts the deep sleep of the giant, who is irked at the leaf, acorn, and droppings of a bird which he believes had glanced off his head. The suppressed anger of Þórr can be gauged by his utter silence and his inability to attack the giant when he reviles Þórr and his companions as *kǫgursveinar,* "small fry," and dares them to seek out the court of Útgarðaloki.

Þórr's misadventures at the court of Útgarðaloki are equally hapless. His companion Loki cannot best Logi, a giant incarnation of wildfire, in rapidity of eating. Hugi, an incorporation of Útgarðaloki's thought, outruns Þórr's servant. Þórr himself cannot drain the sea in a drinking feat and in two successive wrestling matches he is unable to defeat a cat, in reality the Miðgarðssnake, and an old woman, the embodiment of old age. Þórr is left with impotent rage. Útgarðaloki and his fortress vanish as Þórr raises his hammer. The futile raising of Þorr's hammer in a void is a vivid image of his ineffectual readiness to do battle. The giant adversary can be fought only on his own terms. Not only strength but an astute and quickwitted ability to create magical illusions are the insuperable weapons of Þórr's most formidable foes.

Þórr's shaken confidence motivates the following scene, his attempt to slay the Miðgarðssnake. Again Þórr is foiled, this time by a hostile and terrified giant who cuts Þórr's fishing line, just as Þórr was raising the monster to dispatch it to Hel. Again Snorri uses the image of Þórr's hammer raised in a void to express Þórr's impotence to ward off his final encounter with the Miðgarðssnake at Ragnarök. Yet, as in Þórr's adventure with Útgarðaloki, the scene is comical. This time the element of humor is hostility. From the start Hymir is angry at having to put up with a guest, apparently a young boy, who insists on rowing with him to the deep sea to do some fishing. He mocks Þórr: "You will feel cold if I sit out there as far and as long as I am used to" (ch. 32, p. 61), and is upset when Þórr, infuriated at the ridicule, swiftly rows past Hymir's fishing spot and approaches the abode of the Miðgarðssnake. The anger explodes into rage when the Miðgarðssnake and Þórr face each other in an encounter both expect to be the last. The Miðgarðssnake glowers at Þórr, after having swallowed the bait, the head of Hymir's prized ox, and blasts a stream of poison at him. Þórr, enraged, raises his hammer. The scene culminates in the fright of Hymir, a giant turned white, as the ocean swamps his vessel. The episode ends with Þórr's angry wading to shore. Because of the comic structure of the scene there is not a hint of hopelessness when Þórr is frustrated in his attempt to kill a relentless foe of the universe. The keen sense of shame and perhaps despair which initially had inhibited the gods from telling about Þórr's luckless encounter has vanished. The entertainment provided by Þórr's misadventures has displaced the awareness that the existence of the universe is still in jeopardy.

Indirectly, however, by referring to more momentous matters, Hárr, "the High One," a hypostasis of Óðinn, alludes to the seriousness of Þórr's limited effectiveness in guarding the universe. Hárr is about to tell the myth of Baldr's death. He recounts how Baldr's mother sought to ensure her son's life by having all things on earth swear an oath that they would not harm the innocent god, but she neglected to ask the mistletoe, which she considered too insignificant to render the oath. Then Hárr tells of Loki's stratagem to have Baldr's blind brother kill Baldr by tossing the mistletoe during one of the gods' ill-advised games in which they flung at Baldr the objects which had sworn the oath. Gangleri hears of the funeral, of the ineffectual ride to Hel to plead for Baldr's return, and of Hel's deceptive promise that Baldr might come back if everything on earth would weep for his life. After apparently every living thing had wept for Baldr, the messengers find in some cave a giantess who refuses to weep. The giantess was Loki, Hel's father, who is finally unmasked as the gods' implacable foe.

Again the portentous nature of Baldr's death is made palpable by elements of the funeral. Baldr's ship cannot be launched to Hel until a summoned giantess dislodges the ship with such brute force that the earth quakes. Þórr enraged by his own insufficiency kicks a dwarf into the funeral pyre. Þórr's might and Óðinn's power have been effectively checked. Again the gods can only postpone Ragnarök by capturing and binding Loki to a rock. Loki's might is thus temporarily confined, to be unleashed at the cataclysmic outbreak of Ragnarök.

Snorri's description of Ragnarök in the final section of *Gylfaginning* is anticlimactic (chs. 37–40, pp. 70–75). He follows the description of "Völuspá" closely, with one significant exception. The sequence of events as presented in "Völuspá" is reversed. The quotation of "Völuspá" in *Gylfaginning* begins with the preparation of the gods against the imminent onslaught of the giants. In Snorri's account of Ragnarök, an account which precedes the quotation, the giants mount a singleminded assault on Ásgarðr before the gods prepare their brave though futile defense. While the world is collapsing and the giant forces attack in several formations, Óðinn puts on his golden helmet in a symbolic gesture, since the helmet is ornamental rather than a protective piece of armor. He then sets out to meet the giant forces with Þórr at his side. This reversal in the sequence of events has an untoward effect. The grandeur and dignity of the battle so prominent in "Völuspá" are nonexistent. Instead, there is a pervasive sense of futility. The gods perform their duty, as the giants unleash their pent-up fury in a cosmic battle ordained by fate.

In the final chapters of *Gylfaginning* Snorri introduces a variation of a theme central to his account on the origin of the universe, that forces hostile to life engender life. Despite Ragnarök, with destruction wrought on a cosmic scale, a renewed form of existence develops. The earth is reborn; the sun before being swallowed by the wolf bears a daughter; vigorous gods, sons of Óðinn and Þórr survive; Baldr and his slayer return from Hel, and a man and a woman, survivors of the cosmic holocaust, find sustenance. This rebirth and renewal constitute the vindication of the Æsir's rule and achievements. Their descendants reign in the new world with the old symbols of power, Þórr's hammer and the miraculously recovered golden tablets of the golden age. There are only somber intimations that evil has also survived, in the description of the hall at the Strand of the Corpses, a hall filled with poisonous snakes, in the report that the mythic snake of evil is torturing corpses and that murderers and oathbreakers wade though the poisonous rivers streaming from the snake-filled hall.

Gylfaginning's persuasive charm rests, then, on myths told tersely and suffused with human understanding. Yet it is a curious work both in tone and structure. The tone for much of the narrative is serious, befitting the topic of cosmic birth, collapse, and rebirth, and the respect due an ancestral religion. Nevertheless several myths are, despite the gravity of the mythic situation, humorous. They are no longer dramatic events but delusive mythic scenes viewed from the secure perspective of a sophisticated and tolerant Christian.

Structurally the work has only an intermittent unity. The conversation between Gangleri and the three gods generally contributes to the sustaining of interest. Throughout much of the narrative Snorri presents Gylfi and his hosts in a situation of flux, in which the flow of questions and answers suggests the emotions and postures of the speakers. The gods intimidate Gylfi, indulge in mockery, and eloquently display their power of persuasion. Gylfi challenges the gods' assertions of divinity, a challenge obliquely expressed in the directness of his questions and openly in occasional flaunts. This loose structure of questions and answers is, however, not consistently maintained. There are long narrative sections which are preceded only by an introductory question which lacks the emotional and intellectual quality of much of the intercourse. Nevertheless the narrative situation is apposite both as a setting in which questions and answers are easily traded and as a literary reminder that the narrative moves within an authentic, pagan, mythical world.

Also the major themes occasionally are submerged in the narration of myths and mythical facts. This is particularly evident in Snorri's presentation of Óðinn as the major divinity and in attempts to illustrate the precariousness of existence as well as the finiteness of creation. In doing so, Snorri sought to mold mythic narratives and themes into an entity that had no place in tradition. In myths featuring divinities other than Óðinn, the Óðinn-theme, if mentioned at all, is restricted to marginal remarks. The major concern was the narrative integrity of the individual myth, but this necessarily led to the fragmentation of what was to be a unifying theme.

Gylfaginning also lacks completeness. The work contains only select myths. Singularly, not all myths glorifying Óðinn as a culture hero are found in *Gylfaginning*. This can be partly explained by the fact that important myths were recorded in *Skáldskaparmál,* a section probably completed before *Gylfaginning.* Partly, however, these omissions suggest that much of the work was written in haste.

Yet pointing to structural flaws seems akin to caviling. The almost magical appeal of *Gylfaginning* is in its masterful narrative, a narrative of such persuasion that like Gylfi the audience is beguiled. Even the unfamiliarity of the many names and situations fails to irritate. The world of *Gylfaginning* provides intellectual enchantment, for it is a world both remote and well known. We recognize archetypal situations and interrelationships. Also apprehended through Snorri's empathy and imaginative power is a world in which the characters, their achievements and limitations, are singularly and uncannily similar to our own.

III Skáldskaparmál, "Poetic Diction"

It is univerally acknowledged that *Skáldskaparmál* contains mythological and heroic story matter of intrinsic value and passages of great narrative power. *Skáldskaparmál,* however, lacks structure, coherence, and occasionally general interest. In *Gyl-faginning* the dialogue is a felicitous device used with imagination and verve. The dialogue in *Skáldskaparmál*, however, serves a single literary function, the transmission of information. The speakers, the poet Bragi and the giant sea god Ægir, have no traditional relationship to each other. They are awkwardly manipulated puppets. The scenario, the feast at which Bragi entertains and instructs Ægir, remains lifeless, possibly because the lack of a traditional relationship between the speakers inhibited the use of subtle shadings of emotions and reactions. Snorri was a master in reshaping traditional matter, but he needed, so it seems, a well-developed tradition to nurture his art. Consequently, the setting which had a precise function in *Gylfaginning* is discarded in the midst of the work. Bragi and Ægir are dismissed, and perfunctory, rhetorical questions initiate the instructional matter to be memorized by the apprentice-skald.

The beginning of *Skáldskaparmál* contains no clear exposition of the purpose of the work, the teaching of kennings and *heiti*[7] to would-be poets. The myth with which the recital starts out has no observable relationship to the purpose of the work. No kennings are linked to the myth of Iðunn's abduction to giant-land and her perilous return. The subject is briefly introduced in chapter four, after two other myths tangentially related to Iðunn's abduction have been recounted, one of which includes several kennings for gold. Even at this point kennings are only listed during the telling of the myths on the mead of poetry, but no attempt is made to explain the system of constructing kennings. Solely the myths serve as a basis for understanding the traditional kennings on poetry and poetic composition.

Chapter seven contains a cursory introduction to the art of skaldic poetry, the three forms in which men and objects can be described in poetry and a perfunctory reference to the necessity of knowing poetic meters and forms. The purpose of the work is stated only in chapter eight: *Skáldskaparmál* is to teach fledgling skalds the traditional kennings and their formation. Snorri seriously admonishes his readers to esteem kennings used by the great pagan skalds and based on pagan myths and legends. They should be conscious of the fictional nature of these myths and legends. The gods, Snorri points out, were simply Trojans

who after the Trojan War arrogated to themselves divine
attributes.[8]

Structurally *Skaldskaparmál* bears some resemblance to *Gylfaginning*, in the setting and more importantly in the hierarchical
arrangement of the gods and goddesses and the kennings associated with them. Óðinn-kennings head the list, beginning with a
heiti, Allvaldi, "The Ruler of All." Those for Þórr follow and
then those of the other divinities, first male, then female. Extant
skaldic poetry is, however, mainly encomiastic and rulers, warriors, their deeds and aspirations, are objects of poetic praise.
For these reasons Snorri lists and explains the *heiti* and kennings
for a ruler's territories and those useful for the glorification of
exploits and adventures. There are kennings and *heiti* for land,
sea, sky, and the seasons, for battles, weapons, and for the ship,
the traditional vessel for enterprise and exploration. The horse
and scavengers of battle, the raven and wolf, are also accorded
lists of kennings and *heiti*. Of signal interest is the lengthy
section on metaphors for gold. This reflects the importance of
gold as a concrete symbol of political and spiritual power. The
kings and chieftains to whom the skalds addressed their poetry
were expected to be outstanding warriors and patrons of skaldic
art as well as generous dispensers of treasure. Their success on
the battlefield was determined by expertise in strategy and combat as well as by munificence, for fame and generosity attracted
warriors to a court and inspired their service. On a mythical
level, gold was the attribute and gift of the fertility gods and had
to be dispensed to further the peace and wealth that these
deities bestowed on their worshippers.

Snorri cites many kennings for men and women. These usually
reflect man's occupation or social position. One large group, however, incorporates the mythical tradition that man and woman
were created from wooden logs. Man can be poetically described
by referring to him in the first part of a kenning by the name
of a male-gendered tree, and a woman by the name of a tree
having a female gender. The hierarchical order of society was
recognized in skaldic poetry and for that matter by Snorri. He
includes a section on the kennings and *heiti* for members of
social strata, particularly the upper strata of Old Norse society.
Kennings for Christ head the section validating Snorri's in-

sistence that pagan poetic tradition could in good conscience be
cultivated by Christians, since the kennings for Christ showed
that skaldic poetic conventions had been successfully grafted
to Christian religious themes and imagery.

The depth of Snorri's love for skaldic poetry can be assayed
by his masterful command over the poems extant in his era. All
told, Snorri cited 336 stanzas or stanza fragments from sixty to
seventy skalds. Included are what seem to have been Snorri's
favorite poems, Eilífr Goðrúnarson's "Þórsdrápa" and the Eddic
poem "Grottissöngr." Both are poems of singular beauty though
each is composed according to the distinct poetic conventions of
its genre. "Þórsdrápa" is a highly complex and formal poem,
difficult to understand for anyone not exactingly trained in
skaldic poetic discipline.[9] "Grottissöngr" has a bouncy rhythm,
vivid imagery, and a poetic narrative that seems to sweep the
characters to their catastrophic end. Interestingly both poems,
although so different in style, are highly dramatic. "Þórsdrápa"
relates one of Þórr's battles with a formidable giant; "Grottissöngr" is a poem ascribed to two enslaved giantesses working
with a magic millstone. They provide a fortune of gold and then
of salt, and being forbidden to rest they grind a violent death
for both of their insatiable masters.

Skáldskaparmál stands as a monument to Snorri's love for a
complex poetic genre whose existence was threatened by a surging popularity of the entertaining and jaunty dancing ballads.
The work itself bears testimony to Snorri's mastery of the intri-
cate essentials of skaldic composition and to his appreciation of
the best poems preserved in medieval Iceland, including poems
on pagan myths. Also important was Snorri's recognition that
even for poets learning begins with pleasure and that pleasure
provides the motivation for the arduous mastering of what may
seem a lifeless aggregate of factual matter. By writing this
successful textbook, Snorri had sought to preserve and continue
skaldic poetry, and the loose structure of the work reflects this
goal. There is a leisurely guidance to the esthetic beauty of
the tales which underlies skaldic metaphors, quotations from the
best poems produced in the art, and progressively more and more
demanding lists of kennings and *heiti*. *Skáldskaparmál* contributed to the survival of skaldic techniques in modified form.

The essentials of skaldic poetry, the kenning and *heiti* system and metric conventions, were adapted to a new poetic form, the *ríma*, "rhymed ballad." Skaldic poetry was no longer viable even in as traditional a society as Iceland, but skaldic poetic conventions were continued by poets who composed poems with a broader appeal than that commanded by the rigorous, intellectual compositions of the skalds.

IV   Háttatal, "Enumeration of Poetical Meters"

Háttatal is an ambitious work. The poem comprises 102 verses each of which represents a distinct model of skaldic versification patterns and practices. As in *Gylfaginning* and *Skáldskaparmál* the instruction of versification patterns proceeds through judicious questions, correct answers and illustrative verses Snorri had dedicated to Jarl Skúli and King Hákon Hákonarson. *Háttatal* is not only a compendium of existing verses but also includes a number of new skaldic verse patterns. These new verse patterns had, it seems, an important role in Snorri's mission to encourage the creation of skaldic poetry: to demonstrate that skaldic poetry still offered ingenious poets the opportunity to display metric virtuosity and inventiveness.

Snorri was not the first to compose a lengthy poem illustrating skaldic verse forms. An Orkney jarl, Rögnvaldr the Saint, and an Icelandic skald, Hallr Þórarinsson, composed together the poem "Háttalykill," "The Key to Skaldic Metrics," in which they illustrated skaldic versification with verses incorporating heroic legends.[10] "Háttalykill" was the model for Snorri's poem which, however, he may have conceived on a much more grandiose scale. "Háttalykill" comprises now 41 stanzas, Snorri's *Háttatal*, 102.

Despite its traditional format *Háttatal* has no poetic appeal today. Interest in the poem is confined to specialists of skaldic art and discipline.

CHAPTER 4

Snorri's History of the Norwegian Kings to the Reign of Óláfr the Saint: Heimskringla, ca. 1230

I Introduction

HEIMSKRINGLA is the most important medieval work on the history of the Norwegian kings. The name is not given by Snorri but is an editorial name thoughtlessly derived from the opening words of a paper manuscript, *kringla heims*, "the circular world." Serendipitously, the title suggests the intellectual width and breadth of the work in which the Norwegian kingdom with its human, political, and social complexities mirrors the world at large.

Snorri is universally acknowledged as a peerless master in the composition of the *Kings' Sagas*. His design was grand and its execution was structurally and stylistically far superior to any history of the kings composed before his time. The scope of his history was to be large. It was to incorporate the lives of the Norwegian kings from their mythical origin to about 1177. In its chronological span the design was not unique. There were a brief Latin compendium, *Historia Norwegiæ*,[1] and an ambitious Latin work on the history of the Danish kings, *Saxonis Gesta Danorum*. The authors of both works traced the ancestry of the Norwegian and Danish kings respectively to pagan divinities. It is commonly assumed that Snorri did not know *Historia Norwegiæ*, and it is doubtful whether he was aware of Saxo's well-written work. For Snorri's own intellectual circle, the design of *Heimskringla* was of unparalleled magnitude and its composition, a bold experiment in incorporating historical matter of epic tradition into a work with exacting standards of historical truthfulness.

64

The writing of *Heimskringla* was a demanding task, requiring intense intellectual concentration over a period of nearly ten years as well as a huge quantity of parchment. It was therefore a task on a princely scale, princely not only because of the costliness of the undertaking, but also in an artistic sense. The work reflected the strict intellectual standards of a chieftain proud and critical of his heritage and culture.

Composing the *Sagas of the Norwegian Kings* was also an intensely personal matter. From his own experience, Snorri knew that the political independence of his country was imperiled and that it was a matter of time before the Norwegian king would extend his rule to the economically insignificant island on the outskirts of the Scandinavian realm. This insatiable quest for extending political dominion Snorri regarded as a recurrent force or passion in the history of Norway. It was a passion both creative and destructive, creative in that it unified politically the whole of Norway and nurtured an awareness of national identity. The blind destructiveness of this force was palpable in royal opposition to and subjection of any individual and group proud and jealous of personal and political independence.

In *Óláfs saga helga,* "Saga of Óláfr the Saint," this destructive force is described by two historic figures, unlike in character but united in their love for personal liberty and in their fear of political repression. The first is Hrœrekr, a petty king and kinsman of Óláfr the Saint. The second is an Icelandic chieftain, the spokesman for the republic. In one of the famous speeches in *Heimskringla* Hrœrekr warns his fellow kings against recognizing Óláfr as ruler of Norway. Outlining the history of the realm, Hrœrekr points out that each king of Norway with one exception, that of Hákon the Good, concentrated so much power in his hands that the realm suffered. Hence the realm periodically chose to be ruled by the Danish king who, because of geographic distance, assured the chieftains independence and a life of ease. As is usual in *Heimskringla* later events confirmed Hrœrekr's insight. Óláfr had Hrœrekr blinded and some petty kings slain because they were opposed to Óláfr's rule (*Heimskringla II*, chs. 36, 75, pp. 47–48, 105).

Despite a difference in content and detail, the speech of

Hrœrekr is similar in ideological substance to that of Einarr
Eyjólfsson, the Icelandic chieftain. Both emphasize that concentrated royal power leads to loss of liberty and contempt
of human and social values. Yet the tone of Einarr's speech
is more poignant than that of Hrœrekr. Hrœrekr seemed concerned mainly with his own freedom and that of his peers. His
was an egotistical view borne and sustained by his position as
king. Einarr stresses the liberty Icelanders had treasured since
the founding of their republic, a way of life they were obliged
to transmit intact to future generations. He defines the traditional bonds between Icelanders and the Norwegian king which,
if maintained, would preserve political freedom. Icelanders should
continue to bring lordly gifts to the king, hawks or horses, tents
or sails, but should be loath to grant to the king requests which
imply acquiescence to claims of sovereignty, territorial rights
to an island offshore or taxation. Understood by everyone was
the implication that free men bestow gifts on friends or superiors
and that gifts oblige the recipient to extend goodwill and respect
to the donor (chs. 125, 126, pp. 215–18).

Speeches in *Heimskringla* commonly serve to characterize the
speakers and sometimes the audience. Hrœrekr is shown as a
petty king with no vision to guide him in the defense of his
liberty except for a correct assessment of a nonchanging historical force. Einarr, by contrast, is the wise spokesman of the
values a society lives by and lives for. By formulating the island's
commitment to a commonly held political ideal and the consequences of violating the island's political integrity, he staves off
the destruction of a treasured way of life. The entire assembly
accepts Einarr's recommendation as the only course of action.
The subsequent message of the king's emissary confirms the
correctness of their decision just as Hrœrekr's mutilation by
Óláfr corroborated the accuracy of his political judgment. Upon
hearing that the Icelanders denied the king territorial rights to
the island of Grímsey, the king's emissary summoned all of Iceland's chieftains to the king's court. The king intended to
deprive the island of its leadership to further his plans.

Einarr's speech was the last and reluctant commentary on the
king's veiled request for the island's submission. Until he was
asked for his advice Einarr had been silent. His silence during

the favorable discussions on the king's inquiry and his forceful rejection of the king's proposal subtly suggest that he recognized that an ineluctable historic force was undermining the island's republican liberty. This inference is strengthened by Snorri's use of a strikingly modern narrative technique, the use of Einarr's brother as the willing though unthinking advocate of closer ties to the king. The king had directed his request to Guðmundr, Einarr's brother, to the man the king claimed to be the most powerful on the island. Guðmundr seemed willing to accede to the king for the glory and stature that royal favor conferred. This situation was a constant and nagging problem in Iceland's history. Icelanders had traditionally succumbed to the lure of the Norwegian court, an attraction which was nurtured by their instinctual, close contact with Norway. Though politically independent, Iceland depended economically and culturally upon Norway, situated as it was at the periphery of the medieval world. Icelanders hence needed to confirm their stature by recognition at the royal court.

Both the essence of Einarr's speech and Guðmundr's readiness to accede to the king reflect Snorri's irresolvable conflict of the political problem of his time: how to maintain Iceland's political independence in the face of insistent royal expansion and Icelanders' dependence upon royal favor? Icelanders were willing to do the king's bidding to further their own political ends and their detention in Norway by the king came to be a formidable auxiliary weapon in supporting the king's claim. Indeed, Iceland's liberty seemed out of place in the medieval world. That Iceland's autonomy was considered a political anomaly was expressed by the papal legate, six years after Snorri's death. In a missive to Iceland, the legate William of Sabina commanded: "All Icelanders should serve King Hákon, because he [the legate] considered it unheard of that the country did not serve a king like all other countries in the world."[2] Snorri himself did not find a solution to the problem. He acquiesced to the king's claims while in Norway, but refrained from pursuing them in Iceland. Ironically, one of Snorri's farms was the first land to be acquired by the Norwegian king on the charge that Snorri had forfeited it to the crown on account of treason.

Óláfs saga helga, which featured the two speeches on liberty, was the first saga of *Heimskringla* Snorri wrote. This saga is also the nucleus of the chronologically arranged sagas which precede and succeed it.[3] The speeches assume therefore an importance beyond that of their position within the saga. They express a fully formed historical viewpoint. The course of history is determined by an impersonal force, with men acting as its unwitting agents seemingly pursuing personal, religious, or communal ends.

As a major saga of the series, first written as an independent work, *Óláfs saga helga* also exemplifies the criteria which guided Snorri in its composition. He wanted to create a serious history which, given the nature of some of his sources, also had to be an imaginative work utilizing traditional narrative devices to express historic or mythic verities. Snorri realized that discernment was the *sine qua non* for a historian who had rigorous standards for establishing truth and who was also respectful of the mythic truths in stories and tales rooted in the prehistoric past.

Discernment was necessary in the evaluation and interpretation of sources, particularly those from a preliterary stage of society. The sources Snorri valued above all were eyewitness accounts by men of integrity and with historic interest, men who transmitted their knowledge to disciples equally trustworthy and intelligent. He likewise treasured skaldic poems which commemorated contemporaneous events and which often formed a record of a ruler's deeds, as skalds were frequently resident at court and present in battles. Even skaldic poems had to be used with discernment as Snorri emphasized in the prologue to *Heimskringla*, in which he articulated his historical criteria. He pointed out both the limitations of the genre and its basic reliability. Skaldic poetry had to be interpreted correctly, but excessive praise in court poetry was not condign to the genre, since falsification of a ruler's deeds was considered a public expression of scorn. Snorri liberally used skaldic poems in his creation of the past. They were primary sources to be quoted as confirmation of his account or as poetic highpoints. Even descriptive details are based on skaldic stanzas known from and preserved in other historic sagas.

In the prologue Snorri also mentioned songs or poems recited as entertainment. The substance of these songs had been accepted as true by wise and knowledgeable men. Snorri professed that he was unable to vouch for the truth of these songs,[4] yet even before he planned to write Norway's history of the preliterary period, he had to address himself to a problem which would have troubled any serious historian: the pervasive strength of legendary material which expressed mythic rather than historic truth. Before he started to compose *Óláfs saga helga,* he had to decide to what extent he was to employ the mass of legendary material that had attached itself to Óláfr even to the time when Óláfr was a Viking chieftain. These legends were an integral part of the versions of the saga existing at Snorri's time,[5] but this sanctification of all stages of Óláfr's life was contrary to the historic traditions which had been transmitted in Iceland from generation to generation. According to this tradition Óláfr had been a complex man, cruel and vindictive, though without a doubt a great king who was able to inspire loyalty and friendship. Snorri solved this dilemma by portraying Óláfr as a secular king for whom his religious mission, the conversion of Norway to Christianity, coalesced with a hunger for power which would tolerate no opposition. Only after his defeat had begun does Óláfr develop the spiritual and ethical qualities traditionally associated with saints.

The problem of the legendary material that Snorri had to wrestle with also confronted him in the folktales and mythic accounts attached to the early history of Norway. Clearly skalds of note responsible for recording historic events in poetic form had used folktale and mythical material in famous poems. Historians could not ignore cultural traditions accepted as historic truth. Snorri therefore included folktales and myths in his sagas on Norway's prehistoric kings[6] and to a lesser degree in the sagas on the tenth and eleventh centuries. He had recognized that the legends of Óláfr had expressed an essential truth about his complex character, just as folktales and myths articulate in poetic form essential truths about the quality of life and the actions of men. Again Snorri's critical standards affected his mythic and folkloristic narratives. The gods would appear as rulers, human sacrifices would be secularized with the victim's death described as an uncanny and unfortunate accident. Yet,

he carefully retains essential qualities of his tradition. The awe
that myth inspires is present and so are the charm and sophistication of seemingly ingenuous folktales.

II   Hálfdanar saga svarta
"Saga of Hálfdan the Black"

Hálfdanar saga svarta is simultaneously the sequel to *Ynglinga
saga* and the introduction to the sagas on historic kings. As a
historic king Hálfdan fights localized battles against a host of
neighboring kings and chieftains. He establishes an identifiable
territorial base which lends his son the substance and incentive
to unify Norway by force and fear. As a king of the mythic era
Hálfdan has a mythic power of such intensity that the survival
and welfare of his descendants and his realm are ensured.

Kings of the historic era were foremost warrior kings. For this
reason *Hálfdanar saga svarta* begins with an account of the
battles Hálfdan fights to regain the territories that had been lost
after his father's premature death. The saga of his son Haraldr
the Fairhaired, opens in a similar manner. Haraldr, aged ten
and fatherless, has to defend his inherited territory from Hálfdan's
old enemies. The similarities in the opening chapters of the two
sagas serve to purvey both a sense of historicity and a reaffirma-
tion of the verity that the achievements of the father will be
surpassed by the son. Indeed, this belief in inherited character
and in an inherited capacity for attainment is confirmed in a
prophecy toward the end of the saga. A Lapp, a prestigious
sorcerer and patron of Haraldr, announces Hálfdan's death with
advice and a prophecy: "You shall go home [now]. You will
receive the entire kingdom that he [Hálfdan] has had and in
addition you shall gain all of Norway" (*Heimskringla I*, ch. 8,
p. 92).

Hálfdan appears as a king of the mythic era in the second and
last part of the saga. The mythic account of his reign emphasizes
the mana that resides in him and his progeny, as well as the
self-destructive and internecine strain in his kin. Hálfdan is a
model pagan king, powerful, wise, just, and dedicated to the
governing of the realm by law. His luck is patent in the con-
traction of his second marriage. Hálfdan, a widower and

childless, commands a henchman, Hárekr the Magician, to rescue a princess from her forced marriage to a berserk. The dreams of Hálfdan and his queen, a descendant of the famous Viking Ragnarr loðbrók, reveal the regenerative mana of their family line. The thorn that the queen pulled from her shirt, and which grew into an immense tree, presages the birth of Haraldr the Fairhaired. The parallel dream of Hálfdan in which he envisages himself with many locks reveals the prolificness of his progeny. The birth of Haraldr and his swift physical and mental development corroborate the truthfulness of the dreams

Even after death Hálfdan's mythic power is manifest. Each of Hálfdan's territories insists on burying Hálfdan, for they believe that the burial of his corpse would ensure the fertility of the land. In the compromise effected each territory buries part of the body. With this the territorial integrity of the kingship is assured despite the numerous battles Haraldr has to fight against his enemies.

In all mythic accounts in *Heimskringla*, irrational and self-destructive elements are part and parcel of lives endowed with mythic power. In Hálfdan's life this irrational urge is patent in his relationship with Haraldr. Hálfdan does not care for Haraldr. The saga does not explain the antipathy, though somehow it is apparent that this dislike is rooted in the father's jealousy of the son who will someday eclipse him. That this antipathy is oedipal is not only palpable in his mother's deep love for the boy, but also in a folktale scene which will end in the announcement of Hálfdan's death. The folktale is typically Norse. A Lapp sorcerer surreptitiously steals Hálfdan's banquet victuals at Yule, is tortured by the king, and released by Haraldr. The Lapp becomes Haraldr's tutelary spirit who in an understatement typical of Old Norse prose announces sometime after his escape that he is the cause of Hálfdan's death: "Your father complained about a terrible loss when I took from him some food this winter, and I shall reward you [for your help] with some good news. Now your father is dead . . ." (ch. 8, p. 92). Hálfdan's dislike for his son and his uncanny death after a father-son conflict presage on a mythic level acts of internecine warfare that will plague and decimate many of his descendants.

Hálfdanar saga svarta has hence an important mediating

function between the sagas on mythical and historic kings. According to the standards of the historic age Hálfdan is a great king who by his success on the battlefield and wise acts as a lawgiver achieves preeminence and dispenses peace. Apposite to a king of the mythic era Hálfdan's mana is evident throughout much of the saga and manifests itself with particular force after his death. At that time the belief in his mana approximates the trust shown by believers in Hálfdan's divine ancestor Freyr. Freyr upon his death was thought to secure fertility and peace so long as his corpse was in Sweden. For a like reason Hálfdan's body is divided so that his mana would permanently reside in the four parts of the kingdom.

III   Haralds saga ins hárfagra
"Saga of Haraldr the Fairhaired":
The Unification of Norway

In *Hálfdanar saga svarta* Snorri introduced Haraldr the Fairhaired (842–931) as the future military king whose luck on the battlefield would not fail. The introduction of the new era toward the end of the old is characteristic of *Heimskringla*. Nearly every saga, as part of its conclusion, either introduces the succeeding period or points to its problems. The purpose is to convey the paradox of the historical process. On the one hand, there is a historic continuum; on the other hand, historic events occur in a cyclical pattern.

The continuum in *Haralds saga ins hárfagra*[7] is Haraldr's military prowess and ambition. Hálfdan reconquered the large kingdom of his murdered father. Haraldr is the first regional king to attempt and accomplish the unification of Norway. The unification is Haraldr's most important achievement, an achievement regarded by medieval historians as the basis for the Norwegian state of their period. After Haraldr's death, kings with political vision would try to establish themselves as sole rulers of the country, and each king or royal pretender would claim descent from Haraldr, the founder of the united kingdom.

Beginning with *Haralds saga ins hárfagra* strategic, political, and administrative questions have a more dominant role and are answered as well as a medieval historian could. For these answers

Snorri relied as much as possible on his interpretation of pivotal skaldic stanzas dating from Haraldr's reign. In spite of their value as primary sources they had serious defects. They were too fragmentary or the poetic phrasing was too vague to provide sufficient evidence for Haraldr's strategic and political plans. Consequently Snorri supplements the knowledge from skaldic verses with tales in political guise and superimposes on Haraldr's reign the political and administrative conditions of his own time. Modern historians have censured Snorri's procedure and rightly so. Yet this was the only way Snorri and his contemporaries could recreate the grandeur of Haraldr's achievements and could convey the powerful forces which brought about the temporary disintegration of his work.

To appreciate Snorri's accomplishment as a historical writer and recreator of the past, a comparison of Snorri's saga with the text of *Fagrskinna,* a contemporary redaction of *Kings' Sagas,* is instructive.[8] Snorri and the author of *Fagrskinna* describe Haraldr's efforts in human terms rather than depicting Haraldr as a protégé of the giant Dofri, the tutelary spirit of a wild Northern mountain range, as traditional folktales did. In Snorri's brief saga Haraldr's battles become all important. In the first chapter, after introducing Haraldr as King of Vestfold at the age of ten, the series of battles and victories begins with the assaults of his enemies who wish to deprive him of life and land. The perils, however, invite Haraldr to increase his power. By vanquishing his aggressors Haraldr through Guthormr, his guardian, acquires a large enough land base to launch the conquest of the country. Significantly, it is at this point that Snorri interweaves the folktale of the beautiful, proud princess who refuses his offer of concubinage until he has conquered Norway. The story is skillfully introduced to articulate the latent ambitions of Haraldr who, in a skaldic verse commemorating his achievements, is praised as the "sole ruler" of Norway (p. 116). The episode leads to the new phase in Haraldr's rule. He no longer has to defend his realm. He begins to extend it.

In *Fagrskinna's* account there is no notion of a development in Haraldr's rule from a position of defense to aggression. The account opens *in medias res.* After a brief introduction on Haraldr's appearance and character, we see him surrounded by

his loyal retinue. The verses on life at his court characterize him
as a king cognizant of his power and of his ability to maintain
and enhance it by his generosity to his band of fierce and fearless warriors. Some narrative on the conquest follows. The most
serious structural defect, however, is the position and elabora-
tion of the princess tale. The princess tale is not incorporated
sequentially. It is rather a retrospective tale which is appended
to the account on the battle at Hafrsfjǫrðr, a battle which in
Norse historiography finalized the unification of Norway. The
tale has none of the simplicity of the folktale as told by Snorri.
The princess episode is rather a curious amalgam of folktale
elements, Christian sentiments, and miscellaneous laws on sexual
relations. The conclusion summarizes the importance of the tale
for the writer of *Fagrskinna*. The purpose of the tale is elevating
and moral. The girl refuses to give herself to Haraldr because
of her pride. By her wisdom she induces him to issue laws to
protect women from unwanted sexual affairs and to deter them
from entering morally and socially demeaning unions. Since both
the girl and Haraldr are merely twelve years old, their wisdom
is astounding. Yet Haraldr on the same occasion demonstrates
even more forcefully his innate power of insight. In an age which
all listeners knew to be pagan, Haraldr denounces the worship of
powerless gods confined to groves and rocks and swears to uphold the omnipotent God who had created heaven and earth.
In Snorri's account, Haraldr's knowledge of the true God is innate
but vague. In the powerful oath he vows to conquer the country
and swears to the god who created him and rules all things that
he shall never cut or comb his hair until he has conquered the
country or found his death.

The composer of *Fagrskinna* has a limited objective in describing the reign of Haraldr. He wants to present Haraldr from
a Christian perspective. Except for his account of court life
and his citation of skaldic verses, he pays little attention to
political and historic verisimilitude. The conqueror has to be
characterized as a man worthy of esteem. Whereas he lived indubitably in a pagan era Haraldr, the ancestor of Norway's
Christian kings, is endowed with the virtue of insight, an innate
knowledge of God, and the will to uphold his belief about the
nature of God. In his own way Haraldr is also a moral man, since

he conquers his desire for the princess. In vanquishing temptation he becomes a better man and a legislator of correct behavior. Luck is clearly with him or, as the composer of *Fagrskinna*
phrases it: *Styrkti hann hamingja,* "luck supported him" (p. 3).

From a historian's viewpoint Snorri's method of recreating
Haraldr's era must be faulted. Indeed, the stage-by-stage conquest of Norway, as Snorri describes it, is branded as patently
incorrect. Also, some of the battles have a dubious quality.
Several are clearly ahistorical since Haraldr's opponents bear
names which are derived from the districts they head. Etiological
tales thus bolster Snorri's account of a protracted conquest. The
most famous disagreement concerns the battle of Hafrsfjǫrðr.
Snorri and Old Norse historiographers concur that the battle at
Hafrsfjǫrðr signaled the successful conclusion of Norway's unification, whereas historians tend to view the battle as the most
significant but not as the final engagement of the war. There is
also disagreement on the causes of the unification. Historians
claim that the unification resulted from economic forces which
brought about a feeling for national unity and from prior attempts
by other leading chieftains to expand their territorial limits.
Snorri and saga writers in general ascribe the successful unification to one man only.

It is of course difficult to assess how many of his battle descriptions Snorri owes to single tales on the unification of Norway
and how much he owes to his inventiveness. What he does attain
by methods unacceptable to historians is to create in his audience
a feeling for the drawn-out but ultimately victorious efforts
to unify the country. On this historians agree with Snorri. The
unification process was protracted, and Norway's territorial unification was a logical step in the development of the country.

A great king is not only a brilliant military strategist. He
is also responsible for an administration which fosters external
and internal peace. Snorri in his version of Haraldr's rule attempts to measure a historical king against the standards of an
ideal mythological kingship and demonstrates how Haraldr in
some aspects lives up to the norm and in others falls short. The
focal points are Haraldr's stature among powerful, neighboring
kings, his administrative policies, and a personality frailty which

seriously endangers his major achievement, the unification of
the realm.

The stature of a king among his peers is a measurement of
his power within and outside of his kingdom. Implicit is the
understanding that respect by neighboring kings discourages and
inhibits acts of aggression. Snorri narrates two tales which,
beside their intrinsic interest and suspense, have the definite
function of testing the power of Haraldr against the might of
the Swedish and Anglo-Saxon kings. The first tale is about the
Swedish king who plans to wrest from Haraldr not only disputed
border country but, as he vows, even Vestfold, Haraldr's ancestral
kingdom. As in many folktales the instrument of incontrovertible
truth is an old man who in the aristocratic setting of the saga
is very rich and influential. In a reception symbolic of the
respective power of the two kings Áki, as host, provides the
Swedish king with an old and sumptuously furnished hall, but
assigns to Haraldr a newly built hall with costly new furnishings.
At the parting the Swedish king demands an explanation. Áki
replies that the old hall with the old furnishings reflected the
age of the Swedish king, whereas the new hall symbolized
Haraldr's irresistible youth and drive. Thus the tale projects
Haraldr's unrelenting course toward the unification of the realm
and his ability to preserve the integrity of the kingdom during
his lifetime.[9]

The second tale is appropriately placed toward the end of
the saga, for it reflects Haraldr's assertion of independence,
even of superiority, as the Norse sagas claim, to the Anglo-
Saxon king Æthelstan (925–939). The Anglo-Saxon king had
duped Haraldr through an envoy into displaying a gesture of
homage. Haraldr redresses the balance by having his envoy trick
King Æthelstan into fostering his son. In Old Norse sagas the
foster father is customarily socially inferior to the child's father.

Snorri attributes few administrative changes to Haraldr. The
major administrative procedures introduced by him are the ap-
pointments of jarls in every district, the abolition of the allodium,
and the imposition of a tax. The imposition of the tax is considered historical, the abolition of the allodium is not.[10] Both
measures, however, confirm Haraldr's image as a tyrannical mili-

tary leader. They are measures appropriate to warrior kings, who increase power by limiting the freedom of their peers.

Snorri's evaluation of these measures is interesting. He does not relate these measures explicitly to the emigration of powerful and independent chieftains from Norway and to the colonization of Iceland, as is customary in the sagas. Also he does not consider these measures political instruments which aided Haraldr in maintaining the unification.[11] The third measure, however, the appointment of jarls, is shown to be shortsighted. It is the cause for internal strife during Haraldr's long life. His many sons resent the power of the jarls and set out to kill them. Haraldr's policy to maintain solid friendships with the most powerful jarls within the kingdom is therefore unenduring and is a sign of the impending though temporary disintegration of the realm. For Snorri the cultivation of prudent alliances is basic to the preservation of power. When alliances are allowed to break down, as they did in the final years of Saint Óláfr's reign, royal power disintegrates and the land suffers.

This lack of administrative innovations points out the major flaw in Haraldr's political and military achievements. There are no wise provisions for the continuance of a unified realm after his death. Indeed, his love for women and consequently his many sons militate against the preservation of a unified kingdom. Each son feels entitled to his own kingdom and will not suffer any encroachments on his rights. Haraldr's shortsighted solution is to name Eiríkr Bloodax, his favorite son, as successor to the entire realm. As all sons are equal heirs, according to the custom of the land, the appointment was bound to fail. Brothers kill brothers until Eiríkr is driven from the realm.

Again a folktale crystallizes the folly of Haraldr's sexual indulgence which impairs his function as king. King Haraldr falls in love with the beautiful daughter of a Lapp. Lapps in Old Norse sagas are dangerous magicians and King Haraldr's love is plainly uncanny. He is overcome by such blind passion that after her death he would not leave her for three years. The king's madness, which can be cured only by a trick, symbolizes Haraldr's inexplicable lack of concern for the preservation of the unified realm. The sequel to the tale foreshadows the unnatural internecine hate among Haraldr's sons. Haraldr, after his recovery from this madness, detests his sons by this woman so much that he expels them and provides for them only after an appeal to loyalty and reason. This violent hatred among kinsmen is to be a constant theme in *Heimskringla* and is to cause serious disruptions of the peace that pagans and Christians alike had always longed for.

Snorri's use of folktales in describing Haraldr's reign, particularly after the unification of Norway, redounds upon the paucity of historical facts available to him. The folktales have however, a pivotal function. They explain in symbolic fashion the inexplicable mixture of success and failure in a powerful king. Snorri's superimposition of administrative practices of his own time upon the period of Haraldr's reign testifies ironically to his attempt to portray the era as historically as he could. These practices were probably considered old and attributed either by Snorri or by tradition to the prominent figure of Haraldr.

Snorri's overriding interest was to write a coherent and credible account for his contemporaries. This he demonstrates at the beginning of the saga when he, in contrast to the writer of *Fagrskinna,* provides a sequential account of the battles and events which lead to the unification. There was no precedent for this procedure, as far as we know. All Snorri could rely on were skaldic verses and fragmented traditions on the course of Haraldr's military progress. With the little evidence that was available Snorri created a vivid impression of a military man whose imposing personality had such serious shortcomings that they endangered the survival of his military and political achievement, Norway's emergence as a political state.

IV   Hákonar saga góða
"Saga of Hákon the Good":
A Model King

The *Saga of Hákon the Good* is framed by two accounts of treachery and by the description of a land in disarray. The frame, however, is not part of the saga which, in contrast to many sagas in *Heimskringla,* is a self-contained whole beginning with Hákon's elevation as king and ending with his death. This self-contained structure and the external framing in the previous and succeeding saga suggest that his reign is viewed as a model which rulers should emulate and as period of respite from the strife and hostility which all too often burdened the land.

The first period of moral disintegration described in the frame is the ill-fated rule of Eiríkr and the second is the rule of his sons. In Snorri's account Eiríkr's misrule consists of the ruthless killing of his brothers. His motivation is the pursuit of power, yet his disregard of moral considerations is so blatant that his callousness is explained on a mythic level. A tale serves to illustrate the inexplicable, how the best-loved son of Haraldr the Fairhaired could bring the land his father had united to the brink of disaster. The tale relates the circumstances of Eiríkr's uncanny marriage to Gunnhildr, a woman of unsurpassed beauty, who was enthralled by two Lapps. The dominance Gunnhildr will exert in the mismanagement of the country by Eiríkr and later by his sons is foreshadowed in the successful escape from the Lapps, an escape that she plans and executes. When Eiríkr's men find her in the Lapps' hut, she rescues them and herself by sorcery and by pretending to show the two Lapps a sign of affection. After the Lapps had fallen asleep and she had wrapped two sealskins around their heads, she had them killed. This type of procedure, consummate acts of treachery, are to be commonplace in Eiríkr's reign and the reign of his sons. In both reigns she assumes a dominant role.

The tale thus explains on a mythic level the acts of fratricide which Eiríkr subsequently commits. There is no censure of Eiríkr. The only words of opprobrium are perhaps the matter-of-fact adjectives used in describing salient character traits. "He was a violent man, grim, rough, and cold. Gunnhildr, his wife, was . . . most grim."[12] The moral condemnation, however, is implicit in the description of his half-brother's rule; in particular, how Hákon the Good resolves the conflicts of interest besetting every rule. Hákon the Good (948–961) is one of two Norwegian rulers with the surname "good." The byname bespeaks moral superiority and constitutes a judgment on his reign and his relationship to chieftains and peasants.

Með lög skal land byggva, "The country shall be lived in with (or by) the law," is the motto according to which Hákon governs his country.[13] The rule of law thrives in peace and Snorri describes Hákon's reign as a period of peace interrupted only by the incursions of the Danes and of Hákon's nephews. Even his elevation to the kingship is achieved without resort to arms. Hákon arrives from England, where he had been raised, during a time when the power of Eiríkr Bloodax had been seriously weakened. There is no battle. As Eiríkr finds himself abandoned, he sails into self-imposed exile.

Hákon's acts are singularly blessed with luck, luck that seems to be predicated at least partially on moral strength. His peaceful entering of the country redounds upon luck as did his instantaneous alliance with Jarl Sigurðr, the most powerful man in the country. Hákon's luck suffuses his decision to promise the peasantry the abolition of the loathsome law on allodium introduced by his father, Haraldr the Fairhaired. The irresistible force of his claim to the kingship is palpable in the unanimity with which he is accepted as king: "they said that Haraldr the Fairhaired had come there and had become young again" (ch. 1, p. 150).

Hákon's right to rule is visible in his resemblance to Haraldr. Yet resemblance in heathen times meant much more than external likeness. The peasants' judgment implies that in Hákon Haraldr was reborn. This by itself denotes an express acceptance of Hákon's claim to rule, but universal perception of Hákon's moral superiority buttresses his claim. The men from the Uppland district hear quickly that the Trondheim men had proclaimed a king who was in every way like Haraldr the Fairhaired except that Haraldr had enslaved the people whereas Hákon wanted the welfare of all. "That news flew like fire in dry grass to the east and to the farthest corner of the country" (ch. 1, p. 151).

The innate luck of selected members of the royal house combined with moral strength marks Hákon's entire reign. One of his first acts is an act of generosity toward the young sons of his brothers. He makes both of them kings. This is in marked contrast to the policy of Eiríkr Bloodax, who rid himself of all rivals and is censured in *Fagrskinna* as a fratricide. This decision is again an outward sign of Hákon's luck, since by appointing his nephews kings over their inherited districts he wins allies rather than rivals to the kingship. Significantly *Fagrskinna* attributes this act of political daring not to the beginning of Hákon's rule as Snorri had done but to the end, in the seventeenth year of his reign.

In Old Norse literature there is at times a dual awareness, an awareness of the traditions and concepts of the pagan period and simultaneously a Christian awareness which is superimposed on the interpretation of pivotal heathen events. This dual awareness obtrudes itself on Snorri's description of Hákon's rule. Hákon the Good, the first Christian Norwegian king governing a heathen country, is implicitly lavished with the blessings of the Lord. The religious compromises he imposes upon himself spare his reign the internal strife which arises from the clash of opposing convictions.

The preservation of internal peace suggests the invisible yet tangible working of God and His tolerance for a king who under the pressure of circumstances refrains for the good of the country from Christianizing his countrymen by force. Snorri clearly presents the peril to Hákon's reign, as unity is threatened by Hákon's ill-considered vow to assault the peasantry for having forced him to participate in sacrificial festivities. Unity is restored at the outbreak of an invasion by Eiríkr's sons. The same men who had obliged him to join their sacrifices rally to him in defense of the realm. The didactic purpose of the sequence of events is obvious. Internal dissension and bloodshed must be averted to assure the survival of society. Interestingly, despite the emphasis on *góðr friðr,* "the good peace," during Hákon's reign, Hákon is characterized as a great and fearless warrior. In the thick of battle he would scorn the use of helmet and armor and fight visibly in view of the war banner. Indeed, tradition has it that Hákon is killed in his last battle by magic. An arrow shot by a servant boy of Gunnhildr, infamous mother of Eiríkr's sons, wounds Hákon mortally.

Again the dual concept of Hákon's image as a Christian and upholder of peace and his veneration as a warrior king structures the final chapters of his saga. His death is Christian, his burial is pagan. Before dying, he invites Eiríkr's sons to assume the rule. Thus Hákon, in the throes of death, brings about an orderly succession without a trace of hate toward those responsible for his death or toward those opposed to Christianity.

He consents to a heathen burial, should this be desired. Accordingly, Hákon is interred as a heathen king in full armor in a burial mound. A poem commemorating his death describes his welcome as warrior king in Valhalla, the pagan abode of slain warriors. In the poem he has become the symbol of prosperity and the good life associated with his rule. A vision of the devastation and tyranny which follow his death concludes the poem. Snorri does not attempt to resolve this dualism. In the moment of death Hákon reveals an innate magnanimity expected of a true Christian. After his death his people commemorate him as the perfect heathen king, the defender of the realm, the bringer of unity, and the respecter of his people's temples and holy places. As the poem notes: "it is on a good day that a chieftain with such character was born" ("Hákonarmál," stanza 19, p. 196).

V   Haralds saga gráfeldar[14]
"Saga of Haraldr Greycloak":
The Violation of Moral and Secular Law

As Snorri's sagas of the Norwegian kings approach the eleventh century, the accounts of treachery and deception, amorality for the sake of power and in the name of Christianity, increase in quantity and intensity. The reign of Hákon the Good represents in retrospect an interlude when the king, his chieftains and peasants, despite deep differences on the vital issue of religion, would live together as men of good will. What united Hákon the Good and the country at large was an abiding respect for the law.

Disrespect for the law marks the reign of the sons of Eiríkr, led by Haraldr Greycloak, a considerable portion of the rule of Jarl Hákon the Evil, and the five-year term of King Óláfr Tryggvason, Norway's first missionary king. In the *Saga of Haraldr Greycloak* Snorri indicates that the lawlessness of Eiríkr's sons redounded upon frailty of character. In the first chapter Snorri illustrates their character faults, which drive them to violate the law. Eiríkr's sons are rapacious, vindictive, susceptible to slights of honor and, as Snorri alludes to in the first paragraph of the saga, they are perfidious. The perfidy which characterizes their dealings is suggested subtly by the use of a simple and neutral verb in describing a reconciliation meeting: *Ok var þar allt mælt til sætta,* "and reconciliation was pronounced" (p. 198). The verb *mæla,* "to speak, pronounce," is after a complete reading of the saga, a felicitous choice for this typical perpetration of guile. The colorless verb denotes their treacherous *modus operandi,* the fair words which cloak their habitual schemes. Censuring their lawlessness in the detached manner of Icelandic saga writing, Snorri notes: "they did not often keep the laws which King Hákon had set down except those which were to their liking" (ch. 2, p. 204). Snorri ascribes implicitly the misery, sterility, and devastation of the country to their amorality. "The fertility of the land was lost" (ch. 2, p. 203).

Deceit, as Snorri subtly indicated in the first paragraph of the saga, is the hallmark of their political designs and stratagems to enlarge their territory. The motif of deceit becomes pronounced in the third chapter, when Snorri allows Gunnhildr, the queen mother, to assume command of political strategy. Her victim-to-be is the most powerful chieftain of the country, Jarl Sigurðr, formerly Hákon's most trusted friend. The means used to eliminate him are betrayal and the adept manipulation of an inferior man craving self-importance and respect. The enormity of the perfidy is palpable in that Gunnhildr and her sons choose as their instrument Grjótgarðr, Jarl Sigurðr's younger brother. He is less esteemed than the jarl. By promising him his brother's jarldom and by charging that Sigurðr had conspired to make him a little man, they subvert Grjótgarðr's loyalty from his brother to themselves. Grjótgarðr turns informer. On a starlit night, when Jarl Sigurðr visits a farm with a small retinue, Eiríkr's sons, commanding an army, burn down the farm and the men in it. There is no overt censure, only the stark, dispassionate report of the event and the intrigues preceding the act of arson.

Treachery pervades all dealings of the brothers against potential rivals, even against their own kinsmen, whom King Hákon had honored by appointing them district kings. Eiríkr's sons plot a concerted plan to kill Tryggvi and Guðröðr as soon as they suspect them of conspiring against them. The elaborateness and secrecy of the plot against Tryggvi and Guðröðr underscores their perfidiousness. Eiríkr's sons announce that they are going on a Viking expedition, as was their wont. At the point of departure the brothers are so angered during a drinking bout featuring the traditional *mannjöfnuðr*, "a competitive verbal game comparing the stature of two chieftains," that they go their separate ways. That their rage may have been simulated is indicated by subsequent events. One brother and his men sail to King Tryggvi to invite him to join on the Viking expedition. When Tryggvi meets them in a small boat he is assaulted and slain. Meanwhile Haraldr Greycloak surprises Guðröðr at a feast during the night and kills him. The fact that Snorri never allows his audience to observe the planning of the two-pronged ambush dramatizes the nefariousness of the plot as do the ambush in the dead of night, the pretense of friendship and camaraderie, and the subsequent rendezvous of the brothers.

Haralds saga gráfeldar does not end with Haraldr's death. The account of his death is reserved for the following saga, *Óláfs saga Tryggvasonar*, "Saga of Óláfr Tryggvason," which also contains a description of the rule of Hákon the Evil who governed Norway after Haraldr's death. In a formal sense, the conclusion of *Haralds saga gráfeldar* seems arbitrary. Thematically, however, the end of the saga is apposite, for the saga concludes with a summary of the famished, dismal state of the land and of the kings' responsibility for the country's distress (ch. 16, pp. 220–24). By reserving for *Óláfs saga Tryggvasonar* the report of Haraldr Greycloak's death and by presenting the reign of Hákon the Evil as a prelude to Óláfr's rule, Snorri achieves a structural continuity. This structural unity has a moral basis. Underlying the account is Snorri's fundamental condemnation of the treachery perpetrated by these rulers whose use of perfidy has become so lethal that the instrument of their survival turns into a weapon of self-destruction.

VI Óláfs saga Tryggvasonar, "Saga of Óláfr Tryggvason"

A. The Fall of Haraldr Greycloak and the Rule of Jarl Hákon the Evil

Óláfs saga Tryggvasonar[15] opens with an account of treachery and thus continues the theme dominant in *Haralds saga gráfeldar*.

With only brief interludes the theme of treachery pervades major events of the saga: the description of Óláfr's birth and childhood, Jarl Hákon's conspiracies to win Norway and to safeguard his rule from Óláfr, Hákon's death at the hands of a slave, Óláfr's efforts to convert prominent heathens, and Óláfr's death in a sea battle five years after his ascension to the kingship.

The narrative on Óláfr's birth and childhood is traditionally relegated by scholars into a fairy-tale world presented as history. As is common in fairy tales, the hero must fight against overwhelming odds to win the kingdom for which he is destined.[16] Indeed, the account may be read as a folktale in which Óláfr escapes the snares of Gunnhildr and slavery in a foreign country to become by serendipity the favorite of the queen at the Russian court. Yet Snorri lent the traditional folktale elements a historic and fateful perspective. Gunnhildr's treachery and cruelty in ordering that the infant Óláfr, son of the slain King Tryggvi, be killed, is replicated in Óláfr's conduct as king. In the persecution of his enemies Óláfr will be as cruel, clever, and relentless as Gunnhildr had been.

In Old Norse sagas the art of relating synchronous events is undeveloped. Synchronous events must be related sequentially, as if they were separated by time. Snorri attenuates this awkwardness. He presents Jarl Hákon's conspiracy to win Norway in the traditional sequential manner, after his report on Óláfr's childhood and youth, but he unifies the two sections by the theme of treachery. Jarl Hákon's conspiracy is a well-planned and deftly executed scheme of treachery in contrast to Gunnhildr's abortive attempts to have Óláfr slain.

In masterminding the conspiracy to regain Norway following his exile, Jarl Hákon displays a professionalism superior to Gunnhildr's. There is, however, the same contempt of human bonds, the exploitation of human motivation, and the compulsion to serve one's self-interests best. Indeed, in a brief statement in the previous saga Snorri had indicated the consanguinity of the two by commenting that: "a great fondness developed between Hákon jarl and Gunnhildr, but sometimes they harmed each other by perfidy" (*Haralds saga gráfeldar*, ch. 6, p. 211).

The scenario of Hákon's conspiracy recalls Gunnhildr's successful scheme to eliminate Jarl Sigurðr, Hákon's father. Both

exploit the trust placed in kinship and both manipulate their victims' craving for self-importance and power. The difference lies
in the staging. Hákon's intrigue takes place not in a politically
divided Norway, but in the powerful kingdom of Denmark. The
men played off against each other are the famous Danish king,
Haraldr Gormsson, his energetic and power-hungry nephew,
Gold-Haraldr, and Haraldr Greycloak. The confidant of Haraldr
Gormsson and Gold-Haraldr is Jarl Hákon. He encourages on
the one hand Gold-Haraldr to claim half of his uncle's kingdom
and, on the other hand, exhorts the king to resist his nephew's
demands. Concomitantly, Hákon allays the king's fear of com-
promising his royal honor by publicly violating kinship ties.

The pawns in this power game are Gold-Haraldr and Haraldr
Greycloak. Haraldr Greycloak is to be the first victim. King
Haraldr Gormsson had accepted Hákon's counsel that it was
preferable to slay a Norwegian Viking rather than a Danish
nephew. Accordingly the Danish king invites Haraldr Greycloak,
his foster son, to take over the land and fiefdom he had possessed
before he had assumed the Norwegian kingship. In an ambush
by Gold-Haraldr, Haraldr Greycloak is killed. For the first time
Haraldr Greycloak had encountered a disregard of human bonds
which equaled or even surpassed his own.

The nefariousness of Hákon's scheme is underscored in the
sequel. Hákon receives the king's permission to kill Gold-Haraldr.
In order to regain his jarldom and rule over Norway. Hákon
plays on the king's fear of a popular nephew who is to succeed
Haraldr Greycloak and exploits the king's desire for greatness.
With Hákon reinstated as jarl King Haraldr would rule over two
large kingdoms, surpass his father in power, and would be rid
of dangerous rivals.[17]

According to Norse tradition, Jarl Hákon's reign is highly successful until shortly before his death. Upon his assumption of
the rule the fertility of the land is restored, fish return, and the
corn grows once again. He defends the realm against invaders.
He is loyal to his religion and for a long time to the Danish king.
He surmounts the crises which confront him with intelligence,
tenacity, and dispatch. He resolves a conflict of loyalty when he
breaks his allegiance to the proselytizing Danish king rather than
compromise his pagan religion. He rallies his countrymen against

the most renowned and feared warrior group, the Jómvikings, and achieves victory in one of the most famous battles in Norwegian history. He forebears to punish his unloved, contumacious, and illegitimate son Eiríkr for slaying his most trusted associate and for accepting from the Danish king the jarlship over several Norwegian districts. The lack of tensions within the land and the country's prosperity testify to the wisdom and correctness of his rule.

The theme of treachery is resumed only at the end of his life when anxiety over maintaining his power and an uncontrollable susceptibility toward women seize him. At a time when he is blind to the limits of his power and violates the wives of chieftains, he fatefully conspires to have Óláfr Tryggvason, now a famed warrior, lured to Norway. This act of treachery is to be his undoing. Óláfr returns as a revolt against Hákon is under way. Óláfr does not have to fight an arduous battle. Jarl Hákon's son Erlendr loses his life, Hákon's sons Eiríkr and Sveinn flee to Sweden, and he himself is killed by a slave. The tale of Jarl Hákon's death demonstrates on a lower social level the pervasive disregard of human bonds in the service of self-interest. The slave's relationship to the jarl had been close. Both had been born in the same night, a circumstance, which caused the length of their lives to be intertwined. Nevertheless the slave killed Hákon partly because of fright but more importantly in the hope of securing gain.

There is a curious mixture of good and evil in Snorri's account of Hákon's rule. His conspiracy to regain his jarldom and his planned ambush of Óláfr Tryggvason constitute ample justification for the pejorative surname he acquired for an altogether different reason, his staunch support of paganism. Nevertheless, prosperity is the hallmark of his rule and this traditionally denotes the quality of government in a political as well as in a spiritual sense. His death is occasioned by two factors, the excesses he indulged in at the end of his rule and the revelation of God's will. The time for Norway's conversion to Christianity had come.

B. The Cruelty and Deceit of a Missionary King

A sense of triumphant success despite Óláfr's innate cruelty and deceitfulness pervades Snorri's account of Óláfr's meteoric rise. His destiny is to be the first missionary king. His luck in escaping from the bonds of slavery, his esteem at the Russian court, and his ability as a Viking chieftain evidence that he is the man to Christianize Norway, an accomplishment which neither the popularity of Hákon the Good nor the cruelty of Eiríkr's sons had attained. A hermit's prophetic but highly ambivalent judgment of Óláfr's impending missionary activity reflects Snorri's own ambivalence toward the missionary king: "you will help yourself with this and many others" (ch. 31, p. 266). The utterance of course may simply mean that the souls of Óláfr and his converts will be saved. Yet the statement also seems to have a moral intent. The comment might mean that God as judge would have to weigh Óláfr's acts of cruelty against his missionary work.[18]

The themes of cruelty and deceit used toward the enemies of God are introduced even before Óláfr sets foot on Norway and claims the throne. On the journey to Norway, on a brief stop-over in the Orkney Islands, which had been colonized by Norwegians, Óláfr in an ambush forces the jarl to convert with his people or face immediate death and the destruction of their land.

An incident during his bid to take over the Trondheim district affirms that the cruelty evident in his threat to the jarl of the Orkneys is inborn. In a reflex action so swift that it must have been dissociated from forethought, Óláfr, on seeing a handsome man fleeing a ship, grabs a tiller and aims it with such force that it shatters the skull of the victim. The man's handsomeness had been his undoing, for Óláfr had mistaken his prey for Hákon.[19]

The cruelty is perhaps nowhere so blatant as in Óláfr's disposal of Hákon's body. He had Hákon's head carried to an island where thieves and criminals were hanged. He then had the head strung from the gallows, stoned by his army, and reviled with the ignominious and legal designation níðingr, "nithing."[20] In describing the desecration of Jarl Hákon's head, it becomes clear that Óláfr's cruelty is as much an outgrowth of passion as it is an instrument of policy. Cruelty is his most effective weapon in eliminating recalcitrant pagans. During his entire reign the torture killings are merciless. One prominent pagan is bound, his mouth opened, and a snake forced down his throat. In summing up his cruelty, Snorri remarks: "he tormented his enemies, some he burned to death, some he had mad dogs tear apart, some he had lamed or thrown over cliffs" (ch. 85, p. 333).

That God supported Óláfr, though only for a span of five years, is implicit in his success. His acceptance as king is nearly as spontaneous as that of Hákon the Good: "the crowd jumped up and did not want to hear anything but that Óláfr Tryggvason should be their king" (ch. 51, p. 299). His successful attempt to impose his will on the country and to curb at least partially the self-determination of the leading chieftains and their kin is the sole subject of Snorri's political account of Óláfr's reign. He brings the country region by region under a more direct control by persuading or forcing the inhabitants to convert. With political astuteness he concludes strong alliances, with skill he silences or kills leaders of the opposition, and with impunity he destroys idols in the sight of incredulous pagans. He coerces also the sons of prominent Icelandic chieftains to pledge the Christianization of the island in return for their freedom. Indeed, his stature as missionary king is based on a sure grasp of political realities and on a fearless and cruel combativeness undaunted by hardship and magic.

Except for the description of Óláfr's fall, Snorri's Óláfr has little of the glamour attributed to the king in other sagas. He is presented as a man with few personal bonds though in the summary of his personal qualities Snorri states that he is loved by his friends. One traditional and wistful episode highlights the endemic loneliness of those in continuous pursuit of power. One day in early spring Óláfr takes from a peddler an angelica unusually large for the time of the year and gives it to his wife. Contemptuously she slaps his hand, upbraids him for a trifling gift when he should have forced her previous husband to return her possessions. The incident illuminates two facets of life which mar the existence of the mighty. There is no place for gestures of love, for none is expected, a fact which recalls the lack of warmth particularly apparent at critical moments in Snorri's life. There is only time for expanding power to the exclusion of warmth and mercy.

The deprecatory gesture of a woman in misery symbolizes

both the immaturity of her taunt and Óláfr's foolishness in
acting upon it. Her words, reminding Óláfr of the might of her
father, the Danish king, and reproving Óláfr's alleged pusillan-
imity toward her brother Sveinn, reflect not only her lack of
love for Óláfr but also her disregard for basic human values. A
hero had to disprove a taunt even at the cost of his life and her
challenge ultimately leads to Óláfr's death in an ambush. Óláfr
swears to reclaim her possessions and to force King Sveinn to
yield in combat. The fateful foolishness of the oath is apparent.
This will be the sole expedition in which Óláfr summons the
fleet for purely secular and frivolous reasons: the acquisition of
territory without the spiritual backing of a religious cause.

Óláfr's embrace of a secular, egotistical cause coincides with
the rising momentum of an organized opposition toward him.
Snorri relates that many flee to Óláfr's enemy, Jarl Hákon's son
Eiríkr, an accomplished warrior, who is the friend of the King
of Sweden and the brother-in-law of the Danish king. Óláfr's
mortal enemy, the spurned Queen Sigríðr of Sweden, marries
the Danish king. Slowly a mighty and determined coalition is
formed.

In scenes which would normally depict the might and splendor
of a great king, there is instead a mounting sense of foreboding.
The brief description of Óláfr's character prior to the angelica
episode is reminiscent of an obituary notice. His mustering of an
overseas fleet commanded by select warriors from the entire
realm has a resplendent but ominous ring. The warm reception
of Óláfr and his fleet by the Wendish king and his acquiescence
to Óláfr's property claims only heighten the feeling of awe and
imminent danger. The feeling engendered is that the stature and
personality of a man can be appraised best before his fall.

As is typical of saga literature, the warning signs of approaching adversity are visible except to the man marked by death.
In Óláfr's case the blindness toward the ambush into which he
is to be led is signaled by his close friendship with Jarl Sigvaldi,
leader of the Jómvikings and notorious for committing acts of
treachery upon oblivious victims. Snorri declares expressly that
Jarl Sigvaldi is sent to Óláfr by the Danish king. The impending
danger is also adumbrated by the eagerness of many of Óláfr's
men to sail home. A sense of doom and dissolution attaches itself

to Óláfr's diminished fleet, as yet still powerful and resplendent.

Significantly· Óláfr's death results from methods he had so successfully employed in his missionary efforts. He and his select group of warriors sail into a trap set with intelligence and secrecy. Yet ironically his heroic stand in the battle and the valor of his men redeem Óláfr as a man. What is remembered are not his wanton cruelty and wily stratagems, but the glory of a doomed and outnumbered warrior fighting his utmost against the superior force of two kings and a battle-proven jarl. Also remembered is the cowardliness of Jarl Sigvaldi who, after the call of victory, rows energetically to the battle.

CHAPTER 5

Óláfs saga helga
"Saga of Óláfr the Saint"

I Introduction

S NORRI'S *Saga of Óláfr the Saint* is considered the best of his
historical works. This is hardly fortuitous. Saint Óláfr (1015–
1030), the man and his legend, had captured the imagination of
medieval Scandinavians more than any other Norwegian king
before or after his time.[1] His fame was not locally confined. It had
spread to the British Isles, to Constantinople, and even to Bethlehem, where a painting of King Óláfr from ca. 1170 graced the
Nativity Church.[2]

As a historian Snorri was interested in the dual aspect of Óláfr's
character and his work. Óláfr was the successful missionary king
and warrior who had kept at bay until the end of his rule the
most able, powerful, and ambitious king of the Northern hemisphere, Knútr the Great, King of Denmark and England. Of equal
significance was the spiritual and political influence Óláfr exerted
on the affairs of his country even after his death on the battle
field. His sainthood was recognized early. The oppressive rule of
the Danes and the economic sufferings of the realm nurtured the
cult of the king who had fallen, so it seemed, in defense of his
country. Concomitantly, a sense of patriotism and self-interest
commingled with the veneration of Óláfr induced his former
enemies to recall from exile his son Magnús. The son of the
saint and his legal successor was chosen to expel the Danish
oppressors.[3]

At the same time the Church aspired to make Niðaróss, the
burial place of Óláfr, the major city of the kingdom. About
thirty years after Óláfr's death Adam of Bremen testifies to
the saint's fame by referring to the pilgrims visiting Niðaróss

and by describing the pilgrims' route via Denmark. Adam likewise attests to the civic importance of Niðaróss. He calls Niðaróss a great and metropolitan city of the realm.[4] At Snorri's time Niðaróss was a wealthy city which he knew intimately. It was an intermediary of the trade to the North, the seat of the Norwegian archbishop, a center of learning, and the possessor of religious treasures which staggered the imagination of pilgrims and visitors alike. Christ's Church, the cathedral built for Óláfr's glorification, harbored the gilded casket of the saint, a splinter of the Holy Cross, and a silver cross with a height exceeding the stature of an average man.[5] Thus, the self-interest of the leading aristocrats, the striving of Niðaróss and its prelates for a position of eminence, and the Danes' ill-considered and hapless tyranny in Norway conspired to project Óláfr as the patron saint of the kingdom. Óláfr's personality, accordingly, assumed heroic proportions, and divine providence was believed to have guided his life.

The task of presenting a saint, the eternal king of Norway, spiritual successor of Óláfr Tryggvason, was a difficult one. Snorri's judgment on the first missionary king was uncompromisingly harsh. Though politically astute and therefore an efficient instrument of God's will, Óláfr Tryggvason exhibited a cruelty unmitigated by the dictates of divine mercy. His missionary activity was crude and inseparable from the twin purpose of subjecting the country to tighter royal control. To committed pagans Óláfr offered no spiritual or theological values. The sole doctrine he imposed was belief in the one god who had created heaven and earth while the physical destruction of heathen divinities was the object of his single-minded care. Óláfr the Saint exhibits a cruelty as intense as that of his predecessor. At crucial times of his life, however, he also had a spiritual awareness of man's obligation to man, an obligation he wistfully realized he had violated in his pursuit of worldly power. Snorri's portrait of Óláfr the Saint is convincing, not only because he reveals Óláfr as a complex man caught within the contradictions of his life as warrior and his destiny as saint but also because of the pervasive irony Snorri perceives in the divine guidance of worldly affairs. Óláfr's achievement as ruler and stature as saint can be gauged only by understanding that God had harnessed

the energy of a cruel, intelligent, though basically sensitive man
in order to establish Norway as the eternal kingdom of his missionary king.

II Óláfr's Childhood and Youth

As is customary in *Heimskringla*, a major theme of the *Saga
of Óláfr the Saint* is introduced in the previous saga, the *Saga
of Óláfr Tryggvason*. Ostensibly for chronological reasons, Snorri
reports that Óláfr Tryggvason godfathered his namesake when
the boy was three years old.[6] The event, however, also had an
auspicious meaning. It augured the boy's destiny to succeed
the first missionary king and to complete his work. During his
childhood and youth, particularly during his career as a Viking,
this baptismal sponsorship serves also as an implicit reminder that
the secular upbringing of Óláfr and his feats as a marauding
warrior are ironically in keeping with God's plan. The divine
plan can be fulfilled only by a warrior of proven ability who
with a singleminded passion will impose religious unity on
his future realm.

Snorri's description of Óláfr's youth is brief and seemingly
commonplace.[7] Yet the account contains the essential elements
which mark him as a leader, his insistent desire to be dominant,
and his careful training as warrior during his formative years.
There is only one anecdote akin to a folktale which is attached
to his youth. It is a typical Old Norse story of a father-son
conflict and is also found in a similar form in other sagas. The
incident illustrates Óláfr's indomitable will power and arrogance which ironically also prove to be the character defects
which will lead to his downfall as king. The story is similar to
a series of events in *Grettis saga Ásmundarsonar*, in which
Grettir's father asks his rebellious son to perform tasks considered lowly and humiliating.[8] In *Óláfs saga helga* Sigurðr
demands a similar task. Óláfr's stepfather requests that the boy
perform a task unworthy of a chieftain and warrior: Óláfr is
to saddle Sigurðr's horse. Óláfr, however, saddles the strongest
buck in the goats' stable. What is particularly interesting is not
so much Óláfr's recalcitrance but Sigurðr's commentary on the
act. Sigurðr regards it as an open act of rebellion against his

authority and a sign that Óláfr will be more determined and masterful than he. This willfulness is also singled out in chapter three, which presents a short characterization of the hero. Óláfr was: "competitive and vehement in games and wanted to outdo everyone, as was to be expected because of his nobility and birth" (ch. 3, p. 4). The statement expresses clearly that Óláfr felt an inner obligation to be first in command and superior in accomplishments. Also implicit in the remark is confidence in his ability and in his tenacity to achieve the prominence he sought.

The stepfather-son conflict crystallizes not only the contrast in disposition but also the contrast between the two modes of life open to aristocrats in Norway. Sigurðr is introduced as a great farmer and farm administrator. Óláfr's repudiation of a menial task signifies that as a warrior he disdains farm labor. Sigurðr's angry remark that Óláfr's mother would consider her son's rebellion "honorable," refers to the arrogance of Óláfr's act, an arrogance commonly associated with the pursuit of power. His statement, however, also implies that both mother and son share the hope that Óláfr will be king over Norway as his kinsman and namesake Óláfr Tryggvason had been.

Strikingly, a renowned warrior, Hrani inn víðfǫrli, the Widely Traveled, is mentioned in conjunction with Ásta and Sigurðr as the third person who directed Óláfr's youth. Hrani's cognomen refers only to his many and distant journeys, but his second byname, *konungsfóstri*, "the king's foster father," as well as his close association with Ásta suggests that Ásta had entrusted Óláfr's training to a proven warrior. Thus the early chapters have a clear-cut dual function: to project Óláfr's consciousness of his innate leadership and to show that his training was in the hands of a man noted for his warriordom and travels. Simultaneously, Sigurðr's unmartial though productive life as farmer-king is repudiated and ridiculed.

The subsequent chapters contain descriptions of Óláfr's Viking life presumably under Hrani's tutelage, but ostensibly as the leader of his own warrior band and as commander of an army. The lengthy, sometimes colorless accounts demonstrate Óláfr's unswerving desire and ability to establish his reputation as a warrior. That the Viking life provided training for his later

conduct of war in the conquest and defense of Norway is
implicit. More importantly his Viking life is from the beginning
an exercise of kingly leadership and ambition. Snorri avers that
according to Viking custom he was called king, and it is curious
that in the succeeding chapters, whether in deference to Óláfr's
later legitimate title or Snorri's wish to emphasize Óláfr's ambition, Óláfr is regularly called king. Consequently Hrani's role
is deemphasized. Hrani is mentioned only four times, once in
the first chapter of Óláfr's Viking life, later as an ambassador
to England, and as Óláfr's companion upon his return to
Norway. The reference in the first chapter is the more interesting.
Hrani's position as helmsman is essential for governing the
craft but his importance is immediately qualified by the phrase:
"and yet he [Óláfr] was king over the troops" (ch. 4, p. 5).

Óláfr's success is measured simultaneously in his associations.
Þorkell hinn hávi, the famous Jómviking, decides to join Óláfr's
Viking expedition to England. The more important association is
Óláfr's prominent position with King Æthelred. Óláfr is the
rescuer of King Æthelred. In a crucial battle for a bridge close
to London, when the king had lost hope, Óláfr suggests and
carries out the victorious stratagem. After that the two kings
(*konungarnir*), Æthelred and Óláfr, defeat a powerful opponent
of Æthelred, Úlfkell snillingr. It is hardly fortuitous that the
chapter closes with the remark that thereafter the country
largely acknowledges Æthelred's supremacy.[9]

Curiously in the next chapter, the only chapter which precedes
the notice on Æthelred's death, Óláfr's battles in England are
described as if they were Viking raids, although supposedly
he held an official office, the defense of the realm: "King Óláfr
moved through much of the country and imposed tribute or
if he did not receive tribute he made war" (ch. 15, pp. 22).

The ambiguous context of this statement and the violence
referred to constitute the sole indication that as a warrior
Óláfr was inevitably involved in pursuits which endangered the
lives of innocents but which furthered his career as a leader of
men. The singular statement and descriptions of merciless
harrowing as an independent Viking leader serve as a bridge
to and as the basis for Óláfr's retrospective judgment on his

Viking life that he and his men had acted wrongfully and had jeopardized both their lives and their souls.

Toward the end of Óláfr's Viking period, a historical and political exposé is introduced. The historical and political descriptions have several distinct functions: 1) they mark the beginning of Óláfr's transformation from the typical, colorless Viking king to a man with an unmistakable and human personality; 2) the shifting political fortunes demonstrate the instability of life which a strong man with an iron will and God's help can control and even mold.[10]

The shift in political affairs is both favorable and unfavorable to Óláfr's hopes and plans. His Viking life is terminated not only by his deep-seated conviction that he is heir to the realm but also by a worsening of his affairs. His protector, King Æthelred, had died and his exiled sons were inactive and weak.[11] The plan of Æthelred's sons to conquer England was dashed by the inferior number of their army and by King Knútr's efforts to preserve the land his father had conquered. With the abortive invasion, Óláfr's ambitions in England were also thwarted. The promise that he would receive Northumberland as recompense for his support could not be fulfilled.

The guiding principle of Óláfr's Viking expeditions, the attainment of military eminence, is expressed in one of Óttarr svarti's skaldic verses, placed appropriately at the beginning of Óláfr's Viking career: "You have displayed glorious courage" (ch. 4, p. 5). His expeditions take him all over the territory frequented by Vikings—Scandinavia, the British Isles, Frisia, France, and Spain. Only a dream, or rather a revelation in a dream, keeps him from traveling to Jerusalem. Óláfr was told that he should return to his homeland because he was to be the eternal king of Norway.

It is puzzling that Óláfr did not return immediately to Norway after the dream but undertook the campaign to reestablish Æthelred's sons as rulers of England. This is particularly incomprehensible since his main opponent, Jarl Eiríkr, had died and the rule of Norway was divided between petty kings and Eiríkr's successors, his brother Sveinn, also the guardian of Eiríkr's adolescent son Hákon. What the events do make clear, however, is that whatever Óláfr undertook, his interests con-

flicted with those of Knútr the Great, the kinsman of the Jarls
and their overlord. Thus the invasion of England may have been
a test of Knútr's power and Northumberland the rallying
point for his conquest of Norway.

By the thirteenth century the term Viking had become an
opprobrious designation. It referred to a rapacious and violent
man unheedful of Christian and social laws. Accordingly, in
the formative phase of his life, his Viking career, there is little
to suggest that Óláfr would be recognized as a national saint.[12]
His Christian mission and divine blessing are introduced only
toward the end of his Viking life and then only in a dream
which prophesied his future role in Norway: "you will be king
of Norway for all eternity" (ch. 18, p. 25), a phrase which prefigures his eternal rule as martyr king. Divine blessing, however,
pervades the account of Óláfr's acquisition and conquest of the
kingdom. Equally pervasive, however, is the force of his personality, intelligence, and leadership which reveal that he is
also innately endowed to act as God's representative in the
Christianization of Norway.

III   The Missionary and Secular King

The religious theme sets in upon his arrival in Norway. He
happens to land at the island Sæla, a name which meant
"Blessed." That this was felt by Óláfr himself is expressed in
his remark: "he stated that this was a lucky day that they had
landed at Sæla in Norway and said that this was a good omen"
(ch. 29, p. 36).

Simultaneously, an incident at the landing also illustrates
that life is largely directed by personal attitudes. As Óláfr lands
in Norway on the eve of his conquest, he slips when stepping
on land. This is generally a portentous omen, as Óláfr himself
implies in the laconic words: "I have fallen." Hrani, however,
interprets the omen contrary to common conception. Óláfr's
stumbling did not signal the imminent failure of his undertaking, but was an augury which meant that his conquest would
endure: "Your knee has joined you to the land. The king laughed
and said: This may be so, if God wills."[13] This laugh and the
qualified understatement typical of heroes display Óláfr's irre-
pressible confidence in his ability to guide events.

During the early stage of the conquest Óláfr expresses for the first time his spiritual awareness of the insoluble conflict between his life as a warrior and the dictates of Christianity. In a policy speech to his stepfather, Sigurðr sýr, Óláfr rejects his Viking life in religious terms: "I and my men have in many places risked both life and soul. Many a man who was innocent, had to give up his money and some also their lives" (ch. 35, p. 43). Significantly, in the only major battle for the realm, the battle at Nesjar (1015 or 1016), he displays a restraint incomprehensible even to his peace-loving stepfather, Sigurðr sýr. Óláfr refuses to annihilate Jarl Sveinn's battered force. In retrospect Óláfr's refusal appears to be an uncanny expression of prescience. Shortly thereafter, Jarl Sveinn dies in exile. That this restraint is an instrument of policy is suggested also by his merciful treatment of Jarl Hákon. Upon his arrival in Norway, Óláfr had captured Hákon by a martial ruse. Solely upon the strength of an oath, Óláfr releases Hákon unharmed: Hákon is not to battle Óláfr for control over Norway. The potential risk Óláfr had shouldered was grave. Hákon's release might have precipitated a potent threat to the realization of Óláfr's ambition, for Hákon would seek refuge with his kinsman and Óláfr's enemy, Knútr the Great.

That the hand of God is responsible for Óláfr's swift success is palpable only at the beginning and the end of his endeavor. Óláfr lands at the island of *Sæla,* "the Blessed," and fights his decisive battle against Sveinn on Palm Sunday. The decorations on the shields with which his men enter battle are also symbolic of his calling as warrior of God. The shields are mostly white and display the holy cross in gold. Of greater importance, however, is a fact which on a secular level would be designated as luck. The ease with which Óláfr, a landless man, first establishes himself as king indicates that God had guided events and had considered Óláfr worthy of divine protection and favor.

Despite the religious theme which is woven into the account of the conquest, the conquest is conspicuously a secular undertaking. From the moment Óláfr lands in Norway, his purpose is to gain the kingdom he considers his by right of birth. The first act he undertakes is the capture of Eiríkr's son Hákon. That the capture was the first step in the quest is palpable in the oath

sworn by Hákon for his release, an oath by which he relin-
quishes his part of the realm and the right to fight Óláfr. The
reception his mother prepares also illuminates Óláfr's intent.
Óláfr's return home is a state visit. Sigurðr sýr, overseeing the
grain harvest in the fields, is forced by his wife to change into
his royal clothing in order to receive his stepson with honor.
Sigurðr himself realizes the import of his stepson's arrival and
the significance of his wife's royal reception: "and thus it seems
to me, if this will come to pass: those who will oppose this
plan cannot protect their lives or their possessions" (ch. 33,
p. 42). Snorri's characterization of Sigurðr as "the wisest of all
men" (p. 41) confers validity on Sigurðr's assessment of his
stepson's ruthless ambition. Likewise, Sigurðr's change of clothes
from the dress of a farmer to the costly and representative raiment
of a king expresses his preparedness to support Óláfr in his quest.
The farmer-king will function temporarily as diplomat and
warrior or, as his wife phrases it, he must act like a descendant
of Haraldr the Fairhaired rather than in the manner of the
peace-loving ancestors of the family line.

The return scene stresses Óláfr's intent to acquire the kingship,
if necessary, by force. As Sigurðr rides to his farm to greet
Óláfr, he first glimpses Óláfr's war banner fluttering in the wind
and only then Óláfr with his band of twenty well-armed men.
Characteristically, Ásta offers her son men and land. In an
incisive statement of purpose Óláfr discloses to Sigurðr his
long-nurtured ambition. Throughout this statement the emphasis
is on his birthright, his kin, and his hatred for Danish and
Swedish domination. The kingdom is his by right of birth
and inheritance. The domination of the country by the Danish
and Swedish kings is *frændaskǫmm*, "a stain on the honor of
his kin" (ch. 35, p. 44), which must be avenged. That he considers the jarls of minor political importance and does not regard
them as rivals is evident in his designation of their function.
They were solely the defenders of the realm. The statement of
purpose hence stresses that his main enemies are not his
countrymen, the powerful aristocrats Snorri had characterized
as jealous of their power, but foreign kings who thought of
Norway as their spoils.

Sigurðr's wholehearted endorsement of Óláfr's plan and

his promise of support presage the success of Óláfr's enterprise. As a wise man he senses the innate luck of his stepson, but he also recognizes that Óláfr had acquired the mental accomplishments demanded of a leader as well as expertise in war. In his reply to Óláfr, he points out that Óláfr's Viking life had provided him with the requisite experience for leadership in politics, administration, and ways of life abroad. This is also the main point of Sigurðr's argument when he persuades the Uppland kings, his kinsmen, to acknowledge Óláfr as king of Norway. In retrospect Óláfr's successful battles for Æthelred's supremacy assume some prefigurative importance. He is a proven warrior and leader whose success is predicated on his experience on the battlefield and his knowledge of statescraft.

Although Snorri had stressed Óláfr's secular accomplishments as requisites for ruling the country, Óláfr is characterized as a Christian king in his ordinances, missionary work, and in his spiritual striving to be a *rex justus,* "a just king." The earnestness of his desire to be a Christian king of European stature is palpable in the introduction of ecclesiastical laws within his realm.[14] Providentially he constructs a royal seat in Niðaróss, the town in which he is to be revered as martyr king. The seating arrangement of his court likewise discloses his esteem for the Church. Óláfr's ecclesiastics are accorded precedence over the courtiers. Snorri, after first mentioning the location of the King's High Seat, relates next that farther in sat Bishop Grímkell and other clerics. His habit of attending Mass before assuming his daily duties as a ruler also evidences his dedication to Christianity.

His missionary zeal extends both to Norway and the islands in the Norwegian sphere of interest. In Norway he ruthlessly compels pagans to convert by mutilating dedicated heathens and depriving them of their property. Both at home and in Iceland he stresses the correct practice of Christianity. In Iceland, by weight of his command, he forces the abolishment of heathen customs which, despite the acceptance of Christianity, had been expressly sanctioned by law. Henceforth, the eating of horse meat and the exposure of children were illegal. The extent of his zeal is illustrated by his many discussions on questions of Christian practice and in his persistent efforts to

ascertain from reliable and knowledgeable people how Christianity fared in such remote places as the Orkneys, the Faroese
Islands, and Shetland.

In the first chapter on Óláfr's reign, the image of the *rex
justus* is projected. He is king with high regard and intense
interest for law. Snorri relates that he often had the law recited
which Hákon Aðalsteinsfóstri had decreed for the district of
Trondheim and that he settled legal matters not by himself but
with the advice of the wisest and most knowledgeable men. The
Christian aspect of his rectitude is brought out in the unsub-
stantiated remark that Óláfr summons the powerful, socially
base as well as the wisest men in his realm. His modification of
the law demonstrates that sound legal administration continues
to be an indispensable means for governing the country.[15]

The moderation Óláfr had exercised in his treatment of
the jarls suggests that Óláfr had been mindful of the divine
command to practice mercy. During the early days of his
reign Óláfr earnestly attempts to adhere to the principles of
Christian conduct in managing the political affairs of his
country. He partly succeeds in being the *rex justus*. Yet despite
his willingness to spare the lives of some opponents and to
consider the welfare of his countrymen above the political and
personal affronts to his honor, the intolerable strain he imposes
upon himself is evident throughout his dealings with his enemies.
Óláfr is vengeful. The threat of rebellion and the precarious
political state of the borderland also nurture an innate but
submerged violence. The vehemence which occasionally possessed
him can be gauged by a terse, matter-of-fact statement that
Óláfr, seized by rage, was unable for several days to discuss
a political crisis (ch. 90, pp. 132–33). The dramatic tension of
Snorri's *Saga of Óláfr the Saint* redounds partially upon the
portrayal of a man who, torn by his desire to be a *rex justus*,
ultimately succumbs to the constraint of circumstances and
to a virulent vindictiveness.

Despite Óláfr's restraint there is no kindness in the figure
Snorri delineates as *rex justus*. His innate grimness and un-
bending vengefulness vent themselves on the enemies of Christianity.[16] Like his predecessor Óláfr Tryggvason, Óláfr kills,
maims, or exiles obdurate heathens. Even in the early part of

Óláfr's reign, this exercise of heedless cruelty is seen as the seedbed of rebellion. Óláfr's cruel treatment of recalcitrant heathens incites his kinsmen, the petty kings who had lent him support, to plan a revolt. Interestingly, Snorri shows that Óláfr's cruel mutilation of his kinsmen is his sole means to maintain his power. Moreover, from Óláfr's viewpoint, the punishment by maiming is more ethical than meting out death, the standard penalty for treachery. The mutilation is presented, as most acts are, without comment. Only later, after Óláfr had survived the plot on his life by Hrœrekr, his blinded kinsman and prisoner, does Óláfr express his disinclination to order the execution of a relative: "It is true that many have been killed for a lesser offense than Hrœrekr has committed. I am loath, however, to lose the victory over the Uppland kings when I captured the five of them on a single morning and acquired their kingdoms in such a manner that I did not have to be the slayer of any of them, because they all were my kinsmen" (ch. 84, p. 125). Implied is the notion that this stroke of luck was related to his restraint and that his restraint continues to be the foundation of his political power. Though Óláfr does not name God, he obliquely attributes his luck to his adherence to an ethical supernal law.

Yet in two conversations about the fate of Hrœrekr, the fraying of Óláfr's restraint is evident and concomitantly the weakening of the spiritual base of Óláfr's power. Óláfr fears that he might be compelled to order Hrœrekr's death. In a subsequent conversation with an Icelandic merchant about Hrœrekr's fate, Óláfr commands that Hrœrekr be deposited on the farm of a prominent Icelandic chieftain or otherwise be killed. Despite Óláfr's caution that Hrœrekr's death should be the last recourse, Óláfr is unwilling to shoulder the risk of a rebellion with Hrœrekr as the rebels' titular head. That Óláfr's fear is well founded is seen both from his courtiers' advice to dispose of Hrœrekr and from a similar but more serious incident faced by one of his successors. The infant king was confronted by a rebellious faction which hauled Magnús the Blind, a maimed, deposed co-regent from a monastery, in order to conquer the country in the blind man's name.[17]

Snorri's exposé of Óláfr's political risks and of the ethical

choice Óláfr had made simultaneously vindicates and censures
Óláfr's unmitigated cruelty to his kinsman by showing the reduction of a proud and wise man to a grim, consummate trickster
seeking to avenge himself and to win his freedom. Perhaps the
most poignant expression of Hrœrekr's mutilated spirit is his
sardonic statement shortly before his death. Since his capture,
Hrœrekr states, he had never felt so good as when he was
made the owner of a small Icelandic farm in full command of
three servants.

The danger of an eroding spiritual power base is present
throughout the successful phase of Óláfr's reign. The rebellion
which nearly led to the deposition of Óláfr Eiríksson, the Swedish
king, provides, for instance, an exemplary and striking warning
to Óláfr. Simultaneously, Óláfr's restraint, as he suffers the
Swedish king's public affront, illustrates the correct conduct
of a Christian king who is preoccupied more with the welfare
of his people than with the injury his honor had sustained. The
series of episodes belong to the most sprightly and controversial
sections of *Heimskringla*. They are controversial, however, only
in one respect, if one seeks solely to establish historic fact in
a political account which for all its liveliness and realistic
detail contains a moral lesson. The account therefore must be
read on two levels. On one level Snorri relates the acrimonious
political relationship of two kings; on the other level he explores
a king's obligation toward his countrymen and the limitations
of royal power; in particular, limits set to arbitrary and arrogant
selfishness.

The conflict begins with a border dispute with both kings
levying taxes in the same district. Óláfr claims the territory
to be his by right of inheritance; the Swedish king seeks to
collect taxes in a territory which had been ruled by the jarls
of Trondheim, his friends and kinsmen.[18] The right is without
a doubt on Óláfr's side, as the Swedish king is told by the most
powerful Swede on a thing assembly: "He [the king] desires to
subjugate Norway which no other king of the Swedes coveted
before and this creates unrest among many men. . . . But if you
do not agree with our decision [a truce and peace proposal],
then we shall attack you and kill you and shall not tolerate the

turmoil you and your disregard of the law are responsible for" (ch. 80, p. 116).[19]

The lesson is that royal power is dependent upon the support of the people. The welfare of the people transcends personal animosity and ambitions. As is customary in *Heimskringla* a series of tales reinforces the admonition. After the Swedish king unilaterally and wilfully abrogated the peace agreement imposed upon him, he is forced to listen to three tales, one a folktale, the second a tale about a skirmish at sea, and the third a story presented as a legal problem which the king is to solve. The tales are to provide him with a mirror of his foolish, injurious, and self-willed conduct. The first story is about a simple man who lost all his precious furs while chasing an elusive squirrel for the sake of its pelt. In the second story there is a sea battle between a Swede commanding five warships and a Danish merchant fleet of five large vessels. The Swede vanquished four of the ships and acquired much money. When the fifth took to the sea, the Swede with one ship set out in pursuit, lost his ship in heavy seas, and was slain with his men when fifteen Danish ships chanced upon the shipwrecked men. The third tale is about a man who wished to exchange legally articles of unequal worth. The Swedish king is bored by the first story, interested in the second, and is able to interpret only the story dealing with the legal problem. He realizes that he and Ólafr are the two litigants and that by refusing to give Ólafr his legitimate daughter in marriage, he had defrauded the Norwegian king who married instead a daughter born in concubinage. The folktale, however, has to be interpreted to him. He is, so he is told by his most trusted and wisest advisers, the foolish peasant who covets a possession with such blind passion that its pursuit would cost him his kingdom. The truth conveyed by the folktale is evident soon after its interpretation. The Swedes have determined to depose the king. His faithful advisers are able, however, to divide the rule between him and his legitimate son and heir.

The political and moral lesson given to the Swedish king is also a forewarning to Ólafr. The Swedes would not tolerate a royal arrogance which exposed them to risk of war and which prevented the people of the Swedish border country from trading with their Norwegian neighbors. The warning to Óláfr is similar. Arrogance in any form and under any circumstance is intolerable in a ruler.

IV   *The King's Arrogance and Fall*

Óláfr's arrogance reveals itself gradually. It manifests itself in cruel callousness toward the rights and feelings of powerful chieftains as he claims territory populated by Norwegians, lands which were either political entities not under Norwegian jurisdiction or only under nominal Norwegian sovereignty. Óláfr's arrogance in attempting to extend his power beyond the confines of Norway is most evident in his request to the Icelanders to cede to him an offshore skerry or to pay tribute. The episode also discloses a character trait which flaws Óláfr's image as *rex justus*. He is revealed as a cunning man who exploits both his position and the weakness of those men seeking his favor or support. His claim to Iceland is first concealed by gifts and assurances of friendship. Before he relayed his political demands he had sent to the island a large church bell and precious wood for building a church. Simultaneously, he had given many Icelandic chieftains costly presents. The gifts are bribes, to make the Icelanders amenable to a transfer of power and to allow the reduction of a proud republic to a dependency of the Norwegian crown.

The political issue in Óláfr's claim to the Faroese Islands and the Orkneys is less clear than it had been in his quest to subjugate Iceland, though the tactic Óláfr employs in his attempt to exact tribute is similar. Both the Faroese Islands and the Orkneys had been tributary lands at one time or another, but had enjoyed periods of freedom and political independence. Óláfr, nevertheless, forces both the visiting chieftains of the Faroese Islands and the rulers of the Orkneys to accept his claims of sovereignty. He commands the chieftains of the Faroese Islands to attend thing meetings convened, as they realize, to make them accept an imposition of tribute. The gifts he gives them at their departure are no longer a mark of esteem. They are tokens of their dependency. The situation in the Orkneys is more complex. On Óláfr's orders or perhaps by his connivance, one of the jarls, an arrogant and cruel ruler, is slain by a chieftain whom the jarl had marked for killing. A dispute over the division of the land follows. One of the surviving brothers, Jarl Brúsi, a peace-loving man and the rightful inheritor of the land, seeks support from Ólafr. Ólafr compels the jarl to accept his land as a fiefdom of the Norwegian crown. The peace-loving jarl had not found justice, only constraint. The jarl's younger, but more willful, independent, and ambitious brother also sails to the king to press his illegal claim. Despite his prior friendship with Ólafr, Ólafr coerced him to be his vassal. On a thing meeting, with the two jarls in his power, Ólafr makes public the constrained vassalage and settles a legal problem ostensibly within his jurisdiction: He arrogates to the crown a third of the Orkney Islands, the rightful territory of the slain jarl.

Ólafr thus makes a mockery of the traditional reception of chieftains or their representatives by the king. The men detained at his court are free men in name only. They are pawns to effect in person or by their kinsmen an acceptance of the king's territorial claims. The dramatic stories Snorri relates about the anger of Icelanders forced to stay at court and their venturesome attempts to regain their freedom illustrate concretely though tangentially the subversion of the time-honored royal function to receive and treat visiting chieftains with dignity and respect.

Throughout the account of Ólafr's stratagems to gain control over outlying lands, Snorri had emphasized the impotence of the men who voluntarily or upon the king's request had joined him at his court. The constraint verbalized by all whom Ólafr had ensnared evidences the king's tyrannical mind. Ólafr's proclivity to overbearing conduct is most conspicuous in his relationship with his closest advisers and friends and in the grudging agreements he concludes with chieftains braving his displeasure or flouting their power. His associations with friends and potential enemies are equally flawed, for he is unable to gauge in others the incandescent force of personal convictions and to appreciate loyalties which contravene his commands.

There are well-known stories about the bravery of Ólafr's friends in defying the king's will in matters of consequence.

Perhaps the most revealing relate to Óláfr's injunction not
to rouse him from his sleep. Even at times of peril his friends
dare to wake him only by a ruse (chs. 83, 122, pp. 122–23, 210).
Interestingly, a political errand which ultimately results in a
major achievement of Óláfr's reign is initiated by his anger at
a friend who suggests that Óláfr should enter into peace negotiations with the Swedish king. The episode appears to be a
typical *forsending,* "a mission to certain death," which Snorri
restructures to illustrate the grimness of Óláfr and his grudging
willingness to accede to the flattering request of a well-meaning
guest. Bjǫrn stallari, Óláfr's counsellor, reluctantly proposes
upon the urging of harried farmers that Óláfr and the Swedish
king should agree on a settlement of the border issue. Óláfr
in turn decrees that Bjǫrn stallari undertake the mission. It is
clear that this embassy is considered a mission of death. All
facts point to Bjǫrn's doom. The Swedish king hates Óláfr
with such intensity that no one at the Swedish court may refer
to Óláfr except by an epithet of disdain, 'that fat man'. A
Swedish kinsman of Óláfr likewise confirms the peril to Bjǫrn's
life. Jarl Rǫgnvaldr responds to the disclosure of Bjǫrn's mission: "What did you do, Bjǫrn, that the king wants your death?"
(ch. 69, p. 89).

Only a friend of Bjǫrn suggests that the mission might not
be a *forsending,* but a heroic undertaking which will be protected by the king's luck. When Bjǫrn's friend asks the king
to grant them his luck, Óláfr assures them of his protection:
"you shall know this for certain that I want to do this, if that
means anything, and place my luck upon you and your companions" (ch. 69, p. 88). The motif of the king's luck and the
control of his anger for the good of his people have changed
the character of the scene. Instead of being sent on a perilous
mission surmountable only by the hero's luck, a transcendent
force shields Bjǫrn and his companions from failure. Only a
minor shift in emphasis will separate this concept of "royal
luck" from the miraculous power of the future saint.

All these episodes cumulatively and individually suggest
that Óláfr's control over his anger and arrogance is tenuous.
His closest friends fear to incite his wrath even by ignoring
trivial orders for momentous reasons. In confrontations with

potential enemies his arrogance slides into a verbal harshness unacceptable to the chieftains who prized their honor and independence. During the reconciliation proceedings with Erlingr, the most powerful and able man of the realm, Ólafr deliberately insults him and the chieftain class: "and I shall . . . not admit that you barons have an inherited right to the land left me by my ancestors and that I should have to pay an outrageous price for your service" (ch. 60, p. 78). The hostility Erlingr harbors henceforth is evident in a subsequent meeting. In response to the king's demand that he and his men be accorded respect, Erlingr remarks sardonically: "and this I shall also agree to. I shall gladly bend my neck before you, King Ólafr" (ch. 116, p. 193). Erlingr's warning that the service he would voluntarily perform would be the most useful to the king goes unheeded. Likewise, Ólafr takes perfunctory notice of his friends' opinion that Erlingr would be his most effective supporter if he could be the king's trusted friend.

During the last phase of his reign Ólafr's arrogance erupts into uncontrolled anger and cruelty. This unmitigated grimness will herald and cause his defeat on the battlefield, his exile from Norway, and his death during his attempt to reconquer the country. During the successful years of his reign Ólafr had bridled his arrogance. He was deeply aware that he must follow a course of moderation and reason. His innate cruelty is directed only to the enemies of God. Interestingly, even this is deemphasized. We hear that Ólafr put villages to the torch only in the final phase of his reign which he justifies shortly before the end of his life as an act performed in the service of God. "It is a shame . . . that such beautiful buildings shall be burned" (ch. 111, p. 182), Ólafr muses at the time he first contemplates the burning of villages during the height of his reign. Snorri, however, does not charge Ólafr at this time with an act of arson. On the contrary, the obdurate peasants and the king come to terms. This restraint even toward the enemies of God suggests that the success of Ólafr's reign had depended in large measure on his ability to curb character traits which untrammeled were injurious to the kingship but nevertheless were requisite qualities for the maintenance of power. Concomitantly, Ólafr's image in this period of his life, the ruler who was always eager for peace, remains unmarred.

In the series of episodes illustrating the relationship of the Swedes to their recalcitrant king, Snorri had sought to convey a moral lesson together with a political account: The partial deposition was a forewarning to Óláfr that self-indulgence of passion would lead to popular disaffection and civil war. Interestingly, Snorri uses the identical literary device to highlight the character defects of both kings. Their unbearable arrogance is introduced or highlighted by their henchmen. The Swedish king's tax officials arrogantly and doggedly attempt to cow Óláfr into paying tribute levied on the Norwegian border country. Their insolent speech and baseless claims reflect the mindless spite of their king and prefigure the unfounded dislike the king will harbor toward Óláfr. Also, Óláfr's henchmen and associates express the unbearable arrogance which in the later years of his reign bursts forth in instinctive acts of cruelty. The first incident is precipitated by a lowly born man, Þórir selr. Two of the closest associates of Óláfr and finally Óláfr himself instigate the subsequent hostilities. In every single conflict the foremost men of the realm are drawn unwillingly into the conflict, adding to the gathering momentum of disaffection and the growing influence of Óláfr's rival, Knútr the Great, who only at the time of incipient revolt conveys his claim to rule over Norway. Þórir selr had been introduced earlier in Erlingr's sardonic speech. Erlingr states unequivocably that while he is willing to curb his pride for Óláfr, he would not pay honor to Óláfr's functionary, Þórir selr, a man descended in both lines from slaves. The comment on Þórir's ancestry is prejudicial although substantively it also constitutes an ethical barb. In Old Norse tradition slaves are endowed with a slavish mentality. They are ruled by their passions or character defect. Consonant with the tone and matter of royal history Snorri underemphasizes in Þórir the simplemindedness associated with slaves or their descendants. Þórir is intelligent, yet he exhibits in crude form the arrogance which Óláfr up to this period had sought to curb.

The first incident is caused indirectly by the king's order prohibiting the export of grain to the famished North. The direct cause of the conflict, however, is Þórir's willful handling of a test case of the king's power. Equally inept is the conduct of Ásbjǫrn, a young and promising man, whose inexperience and ingenuousness leads him into Þórir's trap. From the very beginning of the account Ásbjǫrn is characterized as a chieftain who has not yet acquired good sense and an ability to judge men and predict their acts. Despite the persistent famine, he insists on celebrating the traditional number of festivals in the usual lavish manner, and despite the king's edict sails to the South for grain. His first meeting with Þórir reveals the arrogance of the king's functionary and his hatred for Erlingr, Ásbjǫrn's kinsman. Þórir's farewell and invitation to Ásbjǫrn to stop by on the sea journey home masks his intent to humiliate Ásbjǫrn. Only the inexperience of Ásbjǫrn, his inability to grasp the hatred and spite of Þórir's comments, explain why on his way home with his ship laden with grain, he injudiciously sails past Þórir's domain. Ásbjǫrn had bought the grain legally from Erlingr's slaves, who were excluded from regulations affecting the realm. Nevertheless, Þórir confiscates the grain. In an excess show of force he deprives Ásbjǫrn of his dignity and honor by mockery and the seizure of Ásbjǫrn's beautiful sail.

By temperament Ásbjǫrn is not a violent man, though he is sensitive of his honor. When he sails south again, he sets out to avenge himself and to end the mockery which haunts his existence. Entering Þórir's hall alone and unrecognized he hears Þórir entertaining the king with a falsified account of their conflict. When Þórir alleges that he cried when his sail was seized, he leaps on Þórir and with hatred surging into strength, severs Þórir's head with one blow.

At this point the king's arrogant implacability is manifest, an implacability that can only be countered with force. He brushes aside a plea for Ásbjǫrn's life from Erlingr's son, a hostage at the king's court. That the king cares little about Ásbjǫrn's motivation is palpable in his statement that he will not brook a diminishing of royal honor and power. At the same time conflicting loyalties will bear upon the course of events as will happen with ever-increasing frequency as Óláfr treats his enemies with relentless harshness.

Ásbjǫrn's life will be saved by Erlingr, but during the few

days in which Ásbjǫrn's life hangs in the balance, a loyal friend
of the king and of Erlingr's son prolongs Ásbjǫrn's respite by
stratagems. The confrontation between Erlingr and the king
is a showpiece of Erlingr's might, self-restraint, and leadership.
Erlingr arrives while the king is in church. In a strategy designed
both to cow and to honor the king, he lines his men on both
sides of the street leading from the church to the farm, sta-
tioning himself and his sons at the door of the farm. After the
king with his retinue had passed through the gauntlet, Erlingr
offers him compensation for Ásbjǫrn's foolish act. The unreason-
able vehemence of the king's response to Erlingr's assumed cour-
tesy is reflected in the compromise urged upon him by the
bishop, a compromise which will produce the seed of Óláfr's
destruction. Ásbjǫrn is to take Þórir's place and assume his
function. Erlingr is absent during the compromise proceedings.
His abrupt departure indicates that the king has abused his
honor. Equally clear, except to Ásbjǫrn himself, is the dishonor
he has suffered by accepting the settlement. Ásbjǫrn, as his uncle
Þórir hundr phrases it, has agreed to be the serf of the king,
the equal of the most despicable man, Þórir selr.

The settlement which took no account of the clannish
sensitivity of the chieftain class contributed circuitously to
Óláfr's death. Ásbjǫrn's repudiation of the agreement led to
his death, which in turn set into motion the time-honored
practice of blood revenge. Ásbjǫrn's mother presents Þórir with
a bloodied spear, the instrument of Ásbjǫrn's death. Spear in
hand, Þórir staggers to his ship unmindful of the bridge and
the sea. He had bound himself to slay the king.

The humiliation and slaying of Ásbjǫrn resulted ironically
in a weakening rather than in the strengthening of the king's
power. Two reluctant enemies, Erlingr and Þórir hundr, had
openly become the king's foes. Both eventually leave their
land to seek out King Knútr. Superficially it seems as if Óláfr
had emerged the victor. Actually the powerful men of the realm
were engaging the support of the most formidable king of
the Northern hemisphere to break Óláfr's hold over the country.

The unrelenting hatred of the king surfaces in the haughty
and brash behavior of his friend and emissary, Finnr Árnason,
who subjects Þórir hundr, prior to his departure for England,

to public humiliation on the thing. The incident illuminates that the chain of hostilities cannot be broken. Finnr first imposes an exorbitant compensation in property claims on Þórir. When Þórir denies owning a costly necklace deemed to be the king's property, Finnr thrusts the point of his spear on Þórir's breast. Þórir hands over the necklace but by stratagems pays only a fraction of the compensation. His parting words are seemingly innocuous: "I am pleased, Finnr, that we shall part. But I shall want to repay this debt in such a manner that both the king and you shall not consider the repayment too small" (ch. 139, p. 252). The king's reply to the news of Þórir's defection is prophetic: "I trust that Þórir will be our enemy, but it seems better to me that he be at a distance from me rather than be in my presence" (p. 253). In Óláfr's final battle, Þórir hundr will pierce Óláfr's breast with the spear that had killed his nephew.

Two subsequent, fateful episodes illustrate that the high-handed insolence of his functionaries is merely an extension of Óláfr's arrogant harshness. The first incident draws Óláfr into concealed enmity with Kálfr, the brother of Finnr and the foster father and stepfather of a young, promising man whom Óláfr had slain. The young man had accepted during the final months of Óláfr's reign a gold ring from King Knútr and in the heedless manner of youth, cherishes the gift so much that he wears it under his sleeve while King Óláfr is his guest. In ordering his death Óláfr refuses to consider the boy's youth, the pleas of the boy's kinsmen and of his own friends, and even his own precarious position. The slaying is presented as a gratuitous, irrational act, for the boy's acceptance of the gift is symptomatic of the disaffection at court and in the country at large.

The second episode occurs during the rout of King Óláfr shortly before he is driven into exile. After a victorious sea battle on Saint Thomas's Day, a henchman kills Erlingr. Erlingr, the only warrior to survive the boarding of his ship, had surrendered without arms. Heedless of the heroic stature of his adversary, Óláfr struck Erlingr's chin with the back of his ax, jeering: "One must brand the traitor of his lord" (ch. 176, p. 317). Instantly, the retainer kills Erlingr, believing to fulfill the king's wish. In a sobering comment Óláfr reveals the con-

sequence of this rash act: his henchman had knocked Norway
out of his hands. Yet his henchman's blow was merely an
extension or culmination of his own outpouring of hatred. He
himself had subconsciously given the signal for Erlingr's fall
and he alone bore the responsibility for his defeat.[20]

During the last phase of his reign, Óláfr's implacable cruelty
had turned not only on the chieftains, but on the peasantry as
well. Before his confrontation with Knútr, in the tenth year of
his reign, Óláfr ordered all villages in the Valdres district burned
as a heathen peasant army gathered to defend its faith. This
grim act of arson signals that he had deliberately violated the
principle of mercy and of peace which he had espoused at the
beginning of his rule. In the final battle against Óláfr, the
leaders censure this mercilessness, as they sum up the reasons
for their opposition. The king had treated his people without
pity. Þórir hundr recalls with wistful dignity his own loss: "I
recall this loss of life. Óláfr had four men killed, all distinguished
by worldly honor and by kin."[21] The simplicity of his words evokes
the wastefulness and senselessness of the killings while the
comment itself implicity calls to mind the individual acts of
cruelty which had done violence to Óláfr's self-imposed duty,
his obligation to be a just king.

The period of defeat represents a continuum during which
an ever-increasing aura of uncertainty, futility, and loneliness
surrounds the king. From the beginning Óláfr's power as the
leader of the comitatus, the warrior corps at his court, erodes,
as King Knútr's wealth stealthily corrupts members of his court.
He can depend only temporarily on those who are exerting
leadership in battle. Uncertainty spreads as no one knows the
timing of Knútr's attack. There is only an ominous certainty
that he is assembling an army headed for Norway. This uncertainty and inability to predict and direct events vitiate Óláfr's
efforts to defend his realm and render them futile. From the
outset his battle plans and brilliant stratagems are foiled. He
cannot sustain the large army he has summoned. Ill-advisedly,
he sails to Denmark with a well-armed and disciplined, though
small, force. Joining his kinsman and friend, King Ǫnundr of
Sweden, he proceeds to conquer the country. Both the assault
and the cruelty of the campaign are ill-conceived, for they un-

leash Knútr's might. Knútr's defense of his home-base will initiate the conquest of Norway.[22]

There is a sense of inexorability in the summoning of Knútr's large army, a feeling intensified by the measured but powerful cadence of a simply worded sentence: "It is said that Knútr sailed with this large force from the west of England and landed safely in Denmark with his entire army..." (ch. 147, p. 274). No storm or mishap caused the slightest disarray of the huge and unwieldy fleet. A skaldic verse, which Sigvatr, Óláfr's loyal friend, composes during his stay at Knútr's court, conveys starkly the ineluctability of Óláfr's fate: "I must apprehend the death of the king" (ch. 146, p. 272).

The size of this army and the fear it inspires are largely responsible for Óláfr's defeat. Óláfr's brilliant battle stratagem, the diking of the river Helgá and the sudden release of its waters, causes only a temporary dislocation of the fleet, the loss of some ships and their crews. The fleet soon regroups. Despite the fact that they had not lost any men, Óláfr and Ǫnundr had lost the battle.[23] Perhaps nowhere else is the futility and the disaster of the undertaking expressed more clearly than in the matter-of-fact advice and commentary of King Ǫnundr, whose counsel is promptly rejected: "I now consider it most advisable to return to my kingdom. It is good to travel home on a reliable cart.... Now I want to propose to you, Óláfr my kinsman, that you come home with me..." (ch. 151, p. 282). The decision taken, to remain together with their most skilled and faithful troops, only postpones the dismemberment of their armies.

The self-interests of the troops contravene the resolve of the kings. The Swedish warriors refuse to court death either by opposing King Knútr's army or by facing the harshness of winter in an alien and rugged land. Even Óláfr's army, the select warrior crews of sixty ships, suffers a major defection. An elderly but powerful kinsman declines to join Óláfr's land march to Sweden and sails with Knútr's connivance through the Danish fleet. This is the first instance of a significant desertion, an event which foreshadows Óláfr's loosening grip on his troops. Upon his return to Norway he himself has to dismiss the major part of his army as he establishes his winter base. By this decision he signals unwittingly the demise of his power.

He will be unable to resummon an army. Chieftains desert him as thing district after thing district acclaim King Knútr, and Jarl Hákon returns to take possession of the land he had once renounced. It is as if a phenomenon common to the accession of a popular king had reversed itself. His countrymen ignore Óláfr and his appeal for troops as they flock to do homage to a foreign but generous king. The disaffection and demoralization of his own comitatus is manifest in the useless conflicting advice they offer Óláfr. Again, Sigvatr summarizes poetically and succinctly the cause of the disarray: "Betrayal has set in" (ch. 168, p. 304).

V　Óláfr's Sainthood: The Humanization of a Warrior

During the latter part of his reign Óláfr had been harsh and relentless without measure. Óláfr's transformation into a man of compassion and understanding, a man who will possess the miraculous and prophetic attributes of a saint coincides with the beginning of his defeat. Paradoxically, his relentless hatred of those who betrayed him abates in moments of reflection, even as treachery gradually engulfs him. He exercises an iron self-control at the moment he realizes that he has to retreat in the face of King Knútr's superior fleet. When he announces that those who wish to follow should prepare to take the land route over Gautland to Norway, one of the most powerful men of his kingdom demurs. Reluctantly, Óláfr allows him to depart. The baron with Knútr's connivance has concerted to sail though Knútr's blockade. Even among friends Óláfr brings himself to forgive breaches of faith and loyalty. He readmits Sigvatr, his skald, a man with incongruous friendships, to his retinue after Sigvatr had stayed during a trading mission at Knútr's court. Likewise, during his exile in Russia, he forgives Bjǫrn stallari for swearing fealty to Knútr. Óláfr solely enjoins Bjǫrn to atone for this act with God. Simultaneously, Óláfr expresses his understanding of the frailties of men. He appreciates the difficulties his friends face as they live among his enemies while he himself is in exile.

The gradual humanization of Óláfr results in tolerance and in the self-disciplining of his will to dominate. It is interesting

that before his last battle, after his return from exile, Óláfr
justifies his past relentlessness by explaining an act of magnanimity: he will not allow the burning of the villages in order
to force the opposing army to disband. Though he has in the
past burned farms with their inhabitants, he has done so for
the sake of God. The farmers had reneged their faith. However,
their treachery toward him does not warrant this harsh measure. That Óláfr's mercy is motivated by his sense of sinfulness
is inherent in a remark made later that he also needed some-
one who would pray for the remission of his sins.

Óláfr's sainthood begins before his death and coincides with
the period of his decline as a ruler. His first miracle begins
with his retreat before Knútr in the last year of his reign.
Like Christ he provides food for his followers. He feeds six
hundred men by making the sign of the cross over pots which
contained two heads of cattle. On the same journey he also
defeats the power of evil in a destructive troll. The heat of
his prayers literally sear the troll into flight. Henceforth, the
region is free of the troll's control which results in the clearing
of a mountain pass which the troll had consistently blocked.

Óláfr's power to heal is also first evident shortly before and
during his exile in Russia. In the two healing episodes, the use
of his hands and religious ministrations effect the cure; in the
first case the singing of prayers, in the second a piece of bread
in the shape of a cross was placed in the mouth of an afflicted
youth. Since Snorri avers that the latter episode was officially
acknowledged as a miracle, Óláfr's acts of healing prefigure his
powers as a saint. Upon his death the blood oozing from his
corpse heals the wounded hand of one of his slayers and re-
stores sight to a poor, blind man.

The last phase of his reign also offers the only evidence
of Óláfr's sense of justice which Snorri had wished to emphasize
when he referred to Óláfr's harsh, punitive measures meted out
equally to the powerful and to the weak. The evidence consists
of a single episode. Bjǫrn, a rich man and a friend of the queen,
falsely accuses a farmer of cattle theft. Óláfr drives Bjǫrn from
his land when he discovers that Bjǫrn himself is the thief. The
intensity of Óláfr's anger at the villainy is suggested by the
remark that only the queen's protection saved Bjǫrn from losing

his life or limbs. That there was little basis for the use of the phrase "the powerful and the weak," is clear in retrospect. The poor or the powerless hardly mattered in a society ruled by aristocrats.

Óláfr's exile offers a sharp contrast to his years abroad as a Viking intent in secret on unifying Norway under his kingship. The year at the Russian court (1029) is spent in contemplation. Snorri expressly states that though Óláfr had always led a pure life and had always been engaged in prayer, his mind turned exclusively toward God when his might began to dwindle. How serious his devotion to God was is evident in the statement that while he was in Russia, he intended to give up his kingship, to travel to Jerusalem or other holy steads and to take monastic vows. It is to be inferred that Óláfr, as a private person, wished to consecrate his life to God, but that as king accompanied by his retainers and friends, he had to consider their insistent urgings to return to Norway and attempt to re-conquer the country. The torture in Óláfr's mind is shown in his indecision, his inability to see a clear-cut course of action, and his plea to God that he reveal his plan to him. Óláfr had given up his desire to rule for the sake of power. Henceforth, his life was governed not by his own will, but by the will of God.

Óláfr's decision to reconquer Norway represents hence God's will. Just as he was told in a dream to acquire his kingdom, he is now ordered to regain the kingdom. Again the dream figure is that of his predecessor and forebear, Óláfr Tryggvason. The dream is remarkable not because of the command to reconquer the country, but because of the inclusion of the unequivocal statement that God had given Óláfr the kingdom. The comment hence implies that Óláfr's life had been directed by God, a presupposition confirmed by his predecessor's parting words that God will prove that the kingdom is Óláfr's by right.[24] That God's proof was not to be a worldly triumph is disclosed by dreams upon Óláfr's arrival in Norway and immediately before the decisive battle at Stiklarstaðir in the year 1030. In the first dream the king seemed to behold the entire world, both land and sea, places known and unknown, populated and unin-habited. His bishop, the only man to whom Óláfr confides his dream, characterizes the vision as holy and remarkable. It is to be inferred that King Óláfr knows that the dream signifies death. Surrounded by a multitude, he choses to ride alone, lost in thought. Though, as Snorri points out, it was his custom to be gay with his men and gladden those around him, Óláfr had turned taciturn. Significantly, Óláfr does not confide the dream to anyone else. The inference is that in a society which believed in the significance of dreams, Óláfr's vision was ominous, an augury of his death and defeat.

The second dream shows Óláfr's imminent death in an unmistakable vision. Óláfr sees himself climbing a ladder to heaven. The second dream serves no longer as a warning. It illustrates Óláfr's contentment with his fate.

Óláfr's awareness of his coming death seems to have made him a man cognizant of sin and mindful of the rights of others. For the first time in the saga, we hear that Óláfr bids his men not to destroy the pastures. When, however, in one instance a farmer's field was trampled down, Óláfr provides the field through God's agency with a better yield. He also forbids his men to plunder, for if they should die in battle, it is best to depart without ill-gained wealth. Moreover, the harm caused by stolen goods exceeds by far their usefulness. The total reversal of the king's attitude is shown in a provision which in retrospect appears to be his last will, a testament of forgiveness in the image of God. He gives a farmer much silver, in part to pay for masses for the souls of those who will die in the battle against him.

Óláfr's realization of death seems to have sharpened his moral concern and makes poignant his efforts to Christianize heathens. Snorri consciously stresses the Christian aspects of the battle and the preparations for the fight. Óláfr has but a small band of trained warriors, the greater part of his army consists of men in search of gain, robbers, and a large number of the poor. Yet twice he refuses the help of men proven in arms because they are heathens. Óláfr, according to Snorri, will fight only with baptized men. Historically, this is regarded as a fictive element, as was indubitably, the Christian battle cry, "forward, Christ's men, men of the cross, king's men." The more brutal slogan is found in an earlier version of the saga: "let's us beat, king's men, hard, hard, the peasantry."[25]

Óláfr the Saint dies a victim of the hatred, revenge, and ambitions of Norway's chieftains just as Erlingr had died, the helpless victim of Óláfr's hatred. The death scene marks him as martyr. Snorri remarks that three wounds had caused Óláfr's death, but this is qualified. Óláfr knows his first wound is fatal, for he cast aside his sword and asked God for help. Nevertheless, his two main enemies, in meaningless gestures of revenge, pierce his body. The subsequent stabbings project Óláfr as a helpless quarry. He is mutilated at the point of death as Christ was on the cross and died after darkness had enveloped the battlefield.[26] The miracles which attend his death prove his sanctity. His blood has the power to heal. When his enemy, Þórir hundr, cared inexplicably for Óláfr's corpse, Óláfr's blood ran on Þórir's wounded hand. The hand healed so fast that it required no dressing. A blind man who fell in the hut hiding Óláfr's corpse gains his vision, after he wipes his eyes with the hand that had been immersed in Óláfr's blood. These are the only miracles Snorri relates at this point though he will cite Óláfr's miracles throughout the following sagas as a reminder of Óláfr's eternal presence.

Although the battle at Stiklarstaðir displays distinctive signs of Óláfr's sanctity,[27] the battle description conforms partially to heroic tradition. From the beginning there is a feeling of gloom, the certain knowledge that the hero will meet his death. His obligation is to reaffirm the value of existence by demonstrating the effulgent virtues of heroic life, to provide in the face of death the supreme test of qualities essential for the preservation of life through war: courage, intellectual control, emotional self-mastery, and a determination to live so fiercely that it explodes in inhuman grimness. The heroic theme sets in even before Óláfr dreamed his second dream and related it to a faithful retainer, Finnr Árnason. The implication is that even without divine revelation, Óláfr and his retinue are cognizant of their imminent defeat. It is incumbent upon Þormóðr, as Óláfr's foremost skald, to invest the defeat with the aura of heroic glory. Upon Óláfr's request, Þormóðr recites a heroic song rousing the army from slumber. The song chosen is "Bjarkamál," a poem describing the fall of King Hrólfr of Denmark, a king whose glory and fame had provoked his betrayal. The choice of "Bjarkamál" is significant. Þormóðr verbalizes not only the coming defeat with its elements of treachery, but also the heroic obligation of the comitatus to reward its king by transforming death into a heroic feat. Þormóðr's request that Óláfr should not abandon him in life or death reformulates the meaning of the song: Óláfr will die like Hrólfr, surrounded by his warriors and friends.

In the battle itself Óláfr fights like a hero of the heroic past. He leaves the protection of the shield wall to participate in the hand-to-hand combat. Both in the ferocity of his fighting and in a terse command, the inhumanity inherent in the calling of a warrior is made manifest. The cruelty is exemplified in one slaying, in the cutting stroke which fells a baron whom he had elevated to his high station. Óláfr cuts across his victim's face, splits the noseguard of his helmet, and cleaves his head beneath the eye. The terse command to kill Þórir hundr, "Þórir the Dog," betrays a ferocity of such intensity, that the wording negates his opponent's humanity: "Beat the dog who cannot be slain with iron" (ch. 228, p. 384).

The savage self-control associated with the professional warrior and his pent-up anger is, however, not displayed by Óláfr but by Þormóðr who in saga literature appears as a particularly fierce, sarcastic, and vindictive warrior. His drawn-out death scene is an exercise in merciless self-control. Toward the end of the battle an arrow pierces the left side of his breast. The vague wording of the arrow's site indirectly suggests Þormóðr's self-control, for at the end of the scene we hear that the arrow was lodged close to his heart. In an attempt to extract the arrow, he breaks off the shaft and seeks help with a naked sword in his hand. He lops off the hand of a man who offers to hide him in return for the gold ring Óláfr had given him. When Þormóðr finally enters a makeshift hospital, the physician bids him to pick up a bundle of wood outside of the house. Only after he has hauled in wordlessly the armful of wood does the physician notice his deathly pallor. He orders the physician, who could not tear out the arrowhead with her tongs, to cut away the flesh. He himself then tears out the arrowhead. He dies after looking at the heartstrings attached to the tongs, commenting that the king had fed him well, for the roots of his heart are still fat.

The account of Þormóðr's death ends the battle description. The climactic position of the account and Þormóðr's reference to Óláfr as the king who had fed him strongly suggest that Þormóðr's conduct is paradigmatic for the warrior class. The savage self-control he exhibits can be acquired only by the loss of sensitivity and humanity. The significance of the Þormóðr episode lies hence not solely in his heroic and fierce confrontation with death, but also in the perspective his way of death provides for judging Óláfr's deeds. Þormóðr's savagery calls to mind Óláfr's acts of cruelty and destruction, but his ferocity also is a reminder of the self-control Óláfr had imposed on the grimness inherent in a warrior's character and existence.

By presenting jointly the saintly and heroic modes of life, Snorri indicates that for Óláfr both forms of existence had an interdependent validity. Both Óláfr's training as warrior and his cognizance of the divine commands to exercise mercy and to preserve peace allowed him to gain, rule, and Christianize Norway. Loss of self-control over his innate cruelty, as political pressures from within and without the country steadily mount, accompany his fall. Concomitantly, his understanding of the frailty inherent in the nature of man deepens as he finds himself instinctively breaking the divine commands he had sought to observe. This understanding is the prime reason for the revelation of Óláfr's sanctity as he seeks asylum at the Russian court. The battle at Stiklarstaðir confirms his sainthood while highlighting and judging the qualities of the heroic mode of life, qualities which forged his destiny as temporal and eternal king of Norway.

In his last speech to his army Óláfr had asked God for victory based on his just cause and for the liberation of his land. God's answer was his recognition as saint and the eventual return of his kingdom to his son Magnús. *Óláfs saga helga* fittingly ends not with the death of the saint and his miracles, but with the harsh repression of the country under the Danes, the disappointed hopes of the aristocracy, the acknowledgment of Óláfr's sainthood, and the move to bring Magnús to Norway as king. Significantly, Óláfr's bitter enemies head the efforts to acclaim Magnús as king, whereas a pretender from England, a self-proclaimed son of Óláfr Tryggvason, Óláfr's predecessor, loses his life in a battle for the kingdom against the Danes. God's testimony to the legitimacy of Óláfr's claims was hence grandiose: Óláfr was eternal ruler while the temporal rule returned to his kin.

CHAPTER 6

Magnúss saga ins góða,[1]
"Saga of Magnús the Good"

I *Introduction*

WITH the *Saga of Magnús the Good* Snorri ushers in a new era in Norwegian history. Óláfr's successors have a moral obligation to honor his legacy. They are to observe the duties and moral restraints imposed on Christian kings. In the saga of Óláfr's son, Magnús the Good, the young king arrives by the trials of his life at a reformulation of a warrior king's function and tasks. A warrior king's goals must be restricted by moral claims. At the end of his life, after experiencing a dream vision of his father, Magnús chooses what is the ultimate sacrifice of a warrior king. Magnús wills his own death and thus avoids killing his half-uncle, Haraldr the Hardruler, in the imminent struggle for sole authority over Norway.

By willing his death rather than succumbing to passionate hatred Magnús had reaffirmed the spiritual strength of Óláfr's legacy. Yet Óláfr's spiritual rule extends not only over his successors but over the realm. Óláfr's death had inspired Norway's leaders to search for and to maintain peace. The striving for peace had therefore a twofold strength. The chieftains would preserve peace while Magnús was young. Magnús by reflecting as a mature man upon his father's fate and glory would abjure conquest for selfish and personal ends.

II *The Reign of Magnús:*
The Arduous Quest for Peace

The Saga of Óláfr the Saint had concluded with a sequel which ended in an outburst of national unity and purpose. Óláfr's former enemies had become his most fervent supporters. They sponsored the official declaration of his sainthood overriding the objections of the Danish regent Álfífa. They also journeyed to Russia to lead Magnús, a ten-year-old boy, to Norway. This spirit of national unity expressed in Magnús' return introduces the main theme of the saga, the reconciling of opposing interests, an obligation conferred upon Magnús and his successors by Óláfr's spiritual legacy.

The reconciliation of the entire country with the boy successor of the king slain in battle against a coalition of aristocrats and peasants, is evident in his progress from Russia through Sweden to the districts of Norway. Symbolic of this reconciliation is what appears to be a chance remark or a conventional statement among a seafaring people: Magnús prepares his sea journey when the ice begins to break in spring. The reference to spring foreshadows the warmth of the reception he will receive as he makes his way to Sweden and Norway. His stepmother, Queen Ástríðr, welcomes him as if he were her own rather than Óláfr's illegitimate son. At a thing-meeting she convenes she offers Magnús magnanimously all she possesses. Immediately she organizes a large army to accompany Magnús despite the misgivings the Swedes have about another Norwegian adventure. Her strong words of support, reminiscent of Ásta's willingness to give all she owned to Óláfr's campaign, implicitly convey her desire to act as the true mother of a warrior king. In Norway the entire country accepts Magnús as king while Sveinn and his followers take to flight. There is no battle for the country. Snorri remarks that "the entire country was happy that Magnús had become king" (ch. 5, p. 11).

From the beginning Magnús displays the independence and decisiveness characteristic of a warrior king. Despite Magnús' youth and, we must assume, his dependence on his advisers, his authority is made clear. He initiates the homeward journey; he and his companions prepare their ships as soon as the ice breaks in the spring. He sails to Sweden to meet his stepmother, Queen Ástríðr. The first chapter does not even refer to the barons, the advisers of Magnús, who had initiated his recall. The total disregard of their presence serves to focus attention on the character Magnús will display in his youth and maturity.

Magnús is independent. He had inherited not only Óláfr's realm but seemingly also his character traits.

The quest for honor and power which had dominated Óláfr the Saint emerge in Magnús as he enters manhood, at a time when also the vindictiveness natural to his kin blindly strikes out. In the beginning of his reign, however, these characteristics are submerged. His advisers lead Norway's foreign policy, and theirs is a policy of peace. Together with their Danish counterparts they conclude a peace agreement between Magnús and Knútr's son, Hörða-Knútr: the two boy-kings of Norway and Denmark were to swear brotherhood and maintain peace during their lifetime. If either of them should die without a son, the male survivor was to inherit land and kingdom. The path for permanent reconciliation between the two countries had been laid.

Already in these early chapters, however, the impermanence of peace and conciliation becomes apparent in a minor theme, the petty quarrels over precedence between Queen Ástríðr and Magnús' natural mother, Álfhildr. The squabbles, immortalized in one of Sigvatr's skaldic verses, convey the hollowness of conflicts involving injured honor, even though similar questions of precedence will arise later in a political and national setting rather than in the homespun milieu of royal shrews.

Simultaneously, in a loose association of ideas, the disagreement between the two women allows Snorri to introduce Sigvatr's retrospective and elegiac verses on Óláfr's reign. These stanzas are a reminder not only of a ruler's function as warrior but also of a king's spiritual and material responsibilities.

> *Ætti drengja dróttinn*
> *dýrðar son, ef yrði*
> *Þjóð mætti fǫ fœðask,*
> *feðr glíkr, konung slíkan.*[2]

> The chieftain of heroes
> would have a glorious son
> if he would be like his father.
> Few countries nurture such a king.

The hope that Magnús would follow Óláfr's spiritual guidance is implicit in the verses. Earlier lines of the same stanza, "I rejoice in your life devoted to the law. This is God's loan," again stress the spiritual values which Sigvatr, as godfather, hopes Magnús will imbue. This section fittingly ends with Magnús' decree that Óláfr's Saint's Day be a legal holiday (ch. 10, p. 21). With this legal act the young king unknowingly had assumed an obligation. He would accept the spiritual guidance the life and death of his father had inspired. This guidance would be Óláfr's legacy to the living.

The following chapters evidence that Magnús in the obliviousness of youth ignores Óláfr's spiritual legacy, in particular his duty to preserve the peace within the land. Instead, he allows his vindictiveness, the urge to gratify his thirst for blood revenge, to interrupt the peaceful governing of the realm. The ease with which this peace is shattered demonstrates the impermanence of the political equilibrium Óláfr's former enemies had miraculously achieved. The longing for blood revenge, harbored by survivors of the battle at Stiklarstaðir, constitutes a threat to the political stability of the country. The strength of this passion shared or appreciated by many warriors is palpable in a series of dramatic scenes in which Magnús is or becomes a major participant.

In the first scene Magnús facilitates the slaying of Hárekr, the first major defector from Óláfr's army. When a retainer stationed close to Magnús catches sight of Hárekr, he decides to kill Hárekr to avenge the slaying of his father. By proffering his ax Magnús had become an accessory to the killing and is therefore as responsible as the slayer for a locally confined period of unrest.[3] The scene is oddly reminiscent of the killing of Erlingr. Óláfr's cruel jab with his battle ax had conveyed to his retainer the subconscious desire to have Erlingr slain. The consequences had been serious. Erlingr's death had knocked the kingdom out of Óláfr's hands. Magnús however, had extended his ax wittingly and had thereby initiated a series of vindictive acts which almost deprive him of his kingdom and which threaten to nullify Óláfr's spiritual legacy.

The communal desire for blood revenge surges forth later as a warrior, who had been wounded at the battle of Stiklarstaðir, presents a judicial matter to the king. Magnús disregards him.

Angered at the prominence of Óláfr's former enemies, the man
breaks out in a preemptory skaldic verse:

> Talk to me/King Magnús
> . . . You love/the miserable men
> who betrayed their king.
> And made the devil laugh (p. 23).

The verse curiously inverts the Christian command to forgive
one's enemies as Óláfr had done prior to the battle of Stiklarstaðir when he ordered that masses be sung for the souls of his
slain enemies. The command in the skaldic verse is, conversely,
to seek retribution. The devil continues to laugh because the
king cherishes traitors. The verse has a profound effect. Magnús
settles the warrior's business and promises him his friendship.

The reminder of the warrior that old scores still had to be
settled, unleashes in Magnús the vindictiveness inherited from
his father. Kálfr, one of the three men who had dealt Óláfr a
mortal blow, has to accompany Magnús to Stiklarstaðir to
point out where he stood when he opposed King Óláfr on the
battlefield. Fearing for his life, though he had been one of
Magnús' most esteemed advisers, Kálfr flees to Scotland with his
retainers and portable wealth. The excess to which the passion
of retribution leads Magnús is illustrated in the brief statement
that Magnús confiscates the property of Hrútr of Vigg, a traitor,
whom Óláfr had ordered slain. In phrasing reminiscent of the
generalized comments on punishments the missionary kings had
meted out to their pagan opponents, Snorri describes the destruction of status and property suffered by Óláfr's former enemies.
Inevitably a revolt against Magnús gathers momentum. The
vehemence of feeling within the country bursts forth in the
peasants' outcry against Magnús' excess: "What does this king
think he is doing when he breaks our laws that Hákon the Good
had instituted? . . . He might suffer the fate of his father and
of other chieftains whom we have killed when we tired of their
arrogance and lawlessness" (ch. 15, p. 26). The seriousness of
the situation is evident in the implicit denial of Óláfr's sainthood and in the incipient rebellion, the gathering of an army in
the region dominated by Erlingr's descendants.

Significantly, Sigvatr in a poetic appeal to Magnús awakens

in the young king the qualities of justice and mercy which will assure him of the surname "the Good." By composing his "Stanzas of Plain Speech" Sigvatr reveals himself as the true spiritual godfather of the king: Magnús must keep the laws his forebears had set down; a warrior must be true to his words; a man, whose confiscated property is handed to the king's friends, feels that the king has robbed him. Magnús' acceptance of Sigvatr's poetic rebuke prefigures the strength of character that he will exhibit throughout the remainder of his reign. From this point on Magnús will strive to maintain his father's spiritual legacy. "For this reason he [the king] was called Magnús the Good."[4] Magnús' determination to be a just king is adroitly suggested in the chapter's last sentence, which ends in *Magnús the Good.*

This striving to follow the precepts revealed by his father's death dominates the rest of the saga and will even determine the timing of his death. In his foreign policy Magnús will attempt to be just. He is equally determined, however, to defend his patrimony and his people. His first major task follows the death of Hörða-Knútr, King of Denmark, in 1042. According to the treaty he had concluded early in his reign Magnús assumes the rule over Denmark. The acceptance of his claim to Denmark reveals the blessing that pervades much of Magnús reign. Óláfr's sanctity and miracles had, among other reasons, persuaded the Danes to confirm Magnús as king (chs. 17–21, pp. 31–36).

The seriousness with which Magnús views his duties as warrior king had first become evident in his intention to pursue his claim to the Danish kingdom. He will fight for his right, even if it will mean the loss of his life. This determination to win and to maintain what was his by right will direct his major decisions and the moral choices he is called upon to make in the few remaining years of his life. As king of Denmark he has to defend the kingdom from the attacks of the Wends. At the urging of the Danish chieftains he sails to the country of the Wends and reconquers a lost earldom around Jómsborg on the Baltic Sea. The second time he faces a difficult choice as he seeks to defend Denmark against a Wendish army which vastly outnumbers his own force. So hopeless is the situation that Magnús is sick at heart. Flight would undermine his ability to fulfill the paramount duty of a king, the defense of his people against attack. The importance of upholding this function even against great odds is revealed in the first of two pivotal dreams in the saga. Óláfr the Saint counsels Magnús to fight. He will follow Magnús into battle against the heathen army. As soon as Magnús and his army hear Óláfr's battle trumpet, they should ride to the attack. The next morning, after Magnús had made public his dream, the entire army hears not a battle trumpet, but the ringing of bells. To Óláfr's retinue the bell sounds like Glöð which Óláfr had given to the Clemens Church in Trondheim.

The battle itself illustrates the psychic and physical force emanating from spiritual beliefs and moral conviction. Magnús fights with the frenzy attributed to warriors of the heathen age. He battles without armor, dressed in a highly visible red silk cloak, and hews down men like cattle. His battle ax, inherited from Saint Óláfr, bears a striking, heathen name, Hel, "goddess of death." The sinister, heathen name of a battle ax wielded by a Christian warrior rivets attention on the battle fury which propels Magnús to the head of his army to slaughter the invaders. Solely the absence of savage ritualistic behavior, the imitative howling of wolves and the biting of shields, differentiates Magnús' battle rage from that of the pagan, berserk warriors. The purpose and effect of the battle frenzy, the gaining of victory by terror, are identical. The battle Magnús fights is brief. Magnús' enemies are paralyzed by fear.

Magnús' dream had presaged the divine blessings which would attend the battle and had revealed the power of Óláfr to aid and protect the living. After the battle this power is reaffirmed in the gift to heal which Magnús, the son of Óláfr, confers. In his search for men to tend the wounded, Magnús bequests healing power to warriors whose hands he finds soft and gentle. Among these men are two Icelanders who are listed as healers in historically reliable Icelandic sources.[5] Óláfr's power, moreover, manifests itself as a force which molds beliefs. The victory inculcates the conviction that because of Óláfr's personal protection, Magnús would never suffer defeat.

A political decision considered unwise by one of his closest, oldest, and most experienced advisers also illustrates Magnús' genuine concern for his Danish kingdom. He appoints Sveinn, a nephew of King Knútr, as jarl to govern Denmark in his

absence. The unwarranted trust which Magnús places in Sveinn
is indicated by a correlation of circumstances. Sveinn is a kinsman of King Knútr and his personal qualities mark him as a
chieftain of stature. Of even greater significance in a society
which believed in inherited character traits is the act of treachery
that Sveinn's father had perpetrated on King Knútr, a betrayal
Snorri alludes to in this saga. Sveinn's subsequent conduct
bears out the validity of the suspicion voiced by Magnús'
adviser. The Danes make Sveinn their king. The holy oaths
Sveinn had sworn and the congeniality and respect he had shown
Magnús had merely cloaked his ambition. Magnús had been
unwise in allowing his concern for the governance of Denmark
to overrule his caution.

In the subsequent battles against Sveinn Magnús is a warrior
king whose luck is predicated on his contractual right to rule
over Denmark and on the spiritual support God and Saint Óláfr
had given him. This is evident in a battle speech in which he
places his trust in God and his father. The final section of the
saga, moreover, suggests persuasively that his luck as warrior
king has a spiritual basis. Despite temptation Magnús will pursue
only morally justified claims. Pivotal scenes are the unveiling of
Magnús' desire to conquer England and his abrupt abandonment of the planned conquest. These scenes demonstrate un-
equivocally that only moral constraint sanctified by religion
will curb the ambition and instinctive violence of a warrior king.
The episode in which Magnús' emissaries present his specious
claim to King Edward is reminiscent of King Knútr's equally
unwarranted demand that he should be king of Norway. King
Edward's response, unlike King Óláfr's, is that of a saintly man.
He vows not to renounce the kingdom that is rightfully his.
Should Magnús invade England, he would not oppose him by
arms, but would force Magnús to have him slain. Edward's
declaration reawakens in Magnús his duty to follow the precepts
of his father's legacy. He would not make Edward a martyr
king as Knútr had unwittingly done to Óláfr. Henceforth
Magnús would not pursue doubtful territorial claims. He would
be, as his father had been at the highpoint of his reign, "ever
eager for peace," content to rule the two kingdoms God had
granted him.

With this scene of renunciation, the *Saga of Magnús the Good* ends, though Magnús' reign would continue for one more year. The reason for this unexpected conclusion is not simply due to the chronological complications which beset Snorri in relating the adventures of Haraldr, Óláfr's half-brother from 1030–1046, when Haraldr will demand half of the Norwegian kingdom. The abrupt ending of the saga toward the end of Magnús reign conveys the importance of the moral revelation Magnús had experienced, an illumination which will unfailingly guide his political and personal decisions. His future acts, narrated in the following saga, illustrate his conviction that he must live in accord with God's moral law.

CHAPTER 7

Haralds saga Sigurðarsonar,[1] "Saga of Haraldr Sigurðarson"

I *Introduction*

THE *Saga of Haraldr Sigurðarson* complements up to a certain point the *Saga of Magnús the Good*, for it deals with the life of Óláfr's stepbrother, Haraldr Sigurðarson, his shortlived joint reign with Magnús after an illustrious career in Byzantine service, and his sole rule over Norway for the twenty years following Magnús' death. Despite similar family characteristics, the two rulers are unlike in temperament and spirit. Haraldr is by all accounts a self-made man. After leaving Norway upon the defeat at Stiklarstaðir he acquired high rank in the Byzantine army and uncountable wealth. With luck and the providential aid given him by Óláfr he made his way back to the North. At this juncture of his life the moral suasion of Óláfr influences his career in that King Magnús offers to share the realm with him rather than commit the crime of battling with a kinsman over worldly rule. In their subsequent quarrels Magnús would also control the murderous hatred that overcame him when Haraldr deliberately attacked his precedence in stature and power. Indeed, Magnús' untimely death is self-willed. Illuminated by Saint Óláfr, Magnús chose death rather than a life that would be haunted by an unavoidable crime: the slaying of Haraldr.

In contrast to Magnús' spiritual enlightenment, Haraldr would succumb to the temptations inherent in a warrior's life. He would be unable to recognize that the errors committed by Saint Óláfr were to provide a warning to his successors. In setting his mind and heart on the conquest of lands to which he had no legal claim, he failed to realize, as Magnús had, that conquest for the sake of conquest was immoral and doomed. His plan to

133

conquer England signaled his imminent defeat. Despite the ominous dreams, which troubled him and visionary warriors of his fleet, he launched the invasion. He died as the Anglo-Saxon king entrapped and decimated his warriors when they were proceeding in a holiday mood to a city which they erroneously believed to be in their hands. The course of events in both sagas strongly suggests that Saint Óláfr's sainthood dictated a redefinition of the traditional concept of a warrior king. Norway needed warrior kings, but not for the sake of national or personal aggrandizement. The only ennobling duty of warrior kings was the tenacious defense of their realm.

II *Haraldr's Youth*

Snorri remarks that few facts are known about Haraldr's youth before he fought at the battle of Stiklarstaðir. Nevertheless, the two episodes he includes in the *Saga of Óláfr the Saint* characterize the boy and youth as a future warrior king. As a child he possesses the fearless vindictiveness and ambition natural to a warrior king. A playful episode reveals Haraldr's bent for war and violence. Óláfr, on a visit to his stepfather's farm, probes half in jest the character of his little stepbrothers. The test demonstrates that Haraldr will be a warrior. As Óláfr pulls Haraldr's hair, the youngster yanks Óláfr's beard. When Óláfr asks what Haraldr wants to own more than anything else, the boy replies: "Retainers . . . so many that they would consume at one sitting the [many] cows owned by my brother Hálfdan." The scene concludes with a prophecy that is articulated as if it were a jest: "In this boy, you will raise a king, Mother" (ch. 76, p. 108).

Also the second episode illustrates a characteristic indispensable in the conduct of war. Haraldr, even as a youth, flaunts his unswerving determination by insisting that he participate in the battle of Stiklarstaðir. Despite his immaturity in years, this determination is backed by mature judgment. Haraldr will survive the battle, as Óláfr recognizes before the battle erupts, and will use the battle as the stepping-stone to a military career.

These two episodes appear to be mere vignettes, to illustrate as always in these childhood scenes the most prominent characteristics of the hero and to show Ólafr as a concerned and thoughtful stepbrother. In a larger sense, however, these scenes serve to direct attention to similarity in character. In an incisively phrased, retrospective judgment a close friend of the stepbrothers comments: "I have never met two men more alike. They were both very wise and most valiant in battle, men who strived relentlessly for wealth and power. They were imperious, complex men, strong and vindictive. Ólafr subjected his people to Christianity and its moral teaching, and punished grimly those who turned a deaf ear. The chieftains did not tolerate his just judgments and equal justice to all and they raised an army against him and killed him in his own territory. For that he was declared holy. But Haraldr fought for his own glory and power and subjected everyone he could to his rule. He accordingly died in the territory of other kings. . ." (ch. 100, pp. 200–201).

A verse composed on Haraldr's flight to Russia after the defeat at Stiklarstaðir ironically and rhetorically questions his ability to win fame: "Who knows whether in the future/ I shall be widely known?"[2] The question allows only one answer. Without fame he would not return. Indeed, the fame and wealth he acquires in Byzantine service is unparalleled. No other chieftain had gained such high rank in Byzantine military service. No other chieftain had amassed as large a fortune in gold. When he returns to Norway his reputation is formidable. He is a great warrior with an accumulation of wealth unmatched in the North.

III Haraldr's Byzantine Service and Return to the North

Many incidents about Haraldr's exploits in Byzantine service are historically suspect. There are two major reasons for assuming that the quality of the historical evidence is impaired. First, Snorri's account differs from a Byzantine source. Secondly, none of the skalds who celebrated Haraldr's battles had served with him there and could personally vouchsafe for the truth of their verses. The saga's version, therefore, owes presumably much to Haraldr himself and, as Snorri professes, to two Icelanders who shared with Haraldr the life of Byzantine mercenaries.[3]

Throughout the account of these years Haraldr is a brilliant

military leader who is soon put in charge of the Varangians,
the Scandinavian military contingent at the Byzantine court.
Yet despite the romanticized and heroized features of the narrative, Haraldr's character is unembellished. A series of dramatic
scenes unveil his character defects, flaws that ironically are
also the basis of his strength and the foundation of his fame.
He owes his military success as much to duplicity and an arrogant sense of honor as to prowess, physical strength, and self-
discipline. A dispute with Gyrgir, a Byzantine general, nominally
Haraldr's superior and a kinsman of the empress, makes it clear
that duplicity is a constituent part of Haraldr's famed wisdom.
Both Haraldr and Gyrgir seek to establish their right to the driest
quarters during a military campaign. A game of tokens is played
to resolve the issue. Each contestant is to mark his token. Whose
token is picked up first, shall receive first choice in selecting
quarters. Haraldr asks to see his adversary's mark, seizes the
first token picked up by Gyrgir, looks at it, and hurls it into the
sea. The token that remains bears Gyrgir's mark.

In the stylistic manner of *Heimskringla* Haraldr's act of
duplicity is not spelled out, as no one but he could give evidence
about it. Nevertheless there is no doubt that his conduct is exemplary of his ability to mold events by his wits and to acquire
thereby success as well as preeminent honor. By mentioning that
in subsequent contests Haraldr had always bested Gyrgir, the
saga stresses the signal importance of Haraldr's quest for honor.[4]
The four siege accounts during Haraldr's service also bear out
that Haraldr, as a military leader, relies on stratagems for
success as well as on fierce and fearless fighting. He conquers
all four towns primarily because he gains access to them by the
exercise of his cunning.

The remainder of his Byzantine service will illustrate Haraldr's
self-discipline, cruelty, and particularly his unparalleled daring
which together with providential luck enables him to escape
from Byzantium with his wealth intact. By relating instances of
Haraldr's self-control Snorri emphasizes the close correlation
between his self-discipline and sense of judgment. There is not
a single instance in this saga in which Haraldr is blinded by
rage. On the contrary, Haraldr refers contemptuously to actions
impelled by anger. To him a man who is unable to master his

feelings displays the mentality of a child. Haraldr maintains this self-discipline even in the heat of a savage battle. He ignores the unfounded taunt of a friend who in fear of defeat accuses him of cowardice. He conquers Palestine without destroying the land by fire and arms. In the second phase of his life this self-control and moral self-restraint will characterize his dealings with Magnús the Good. Haraldr will be loath to battle his nephew for the part of Norway which he considers his own.

Haraldr's acts of cruelty and his return to Norway via Russia are both related to adversity. He is accused of having misappropriated the emperor's share of booty and is thrown into prison with two Icelandic companions. According to the saga the true reason for his disgrace and imprisonment is romantic. The empress had fallen in love with him and in anger had first refused to marry her niece to him and had then forbidden him to leave her realm. His rescue from prison is miraculous. Upon Saint Óláfr's command a lady hauls Haraldr and his companions from the dungeon. Haraldr executes the first acts of cruelty attributed to him after his release. During a palace rebellion by the Varangians he blinds the emperor. Then Haraldr briefly abducts an imperial niece and sends her back with a mocking note to the empress. These acts of cruelty are paradigmatic and elucidate the harshness with which he will strike out against enemies once he is king of all of Norway. He is the only king on whom posterity bestowed the byname "Hardruler."

His departure from Byzantium demonstrates the resolute daring which contributed to his awesome reputation as warrior. He orders his two ships to ride up the iron chain which closed off the harbor and his route of escape. He then commands each man to leap with his possessions clutched in his arms to the front of the ship to jolt the vessel over the chain. The ship with Haraldr on board bounces off the chain, the other vessel breaks apart. His escape is the first step in his plan to return to Scandinavia and to gain royal power in Norway.

IV *Joint Rule with Magnús:*
The Fragility of Shared Honor and Power

Haraldr's return to Norway initiates a period of joint rule between him and Magnús, a period of cooperation which is to

become the model for succeeding kings (1046–1047). That
Haraldr had expected Magnús to oppose his claim to the kingdom
is evident in his first alliance. Rather than approach Magnús with
his demand, Haraldr allies himself with Jarl Sveinn of Denmark,
Magnús' enemy. Magnús, however, is magnanimous. Cognizant
of Óláfr's spiritual legacy and Haraldr's military prowess, he
extends to Haraldr a clandestine offer that he should share his
realm. Prompted by his own insights and the counsel of his
friends Magnús had decided that he would not hurl the spear of
death at his kinsman.

This resolve to uphold the obligations of kinship despite the
inevitable strain determines the actions of both Magnús and
Haraldr. The ceremony in which Magnús confers half of Norway
to Haraldr illustrates their good will as well as the unexpected
but deep fissures their relationship would suffer. By handing
Haraldr a slim reed Magnús bestows on Haraldr half of the realm.
Haraldr in turn gives Magnús half of his wealth in gold. The
fragility which flaws the spirit of magnanimity is immediately
exposed, as a jest turns a seemingly innocuous gesture into a
symbol of abiding animosity. Banteringly Haraldr demands that
Magnús offer him a gift commensurate with the worth of a huge
lump of gold. Magnús, impoverished by wars, can offer him only
a gold ring he had inherited from Óláfr. Unknown to Magnús the
ring arouses in Haraldr a wave of hatred for Óláfr had extracted
this heirloom from Haraldr's father in settlement of a minor
legal dispute. The sudden eruption of anger hastily suppressed
conveys the unsettling presentiment that attitudes rooted in the
past and reinforced daily are a constant threat to the cooperation Magnús and Haraldr wish to maintain.

When offering Haraldr half of the kingdom Magnús had followed the precepts which he had set as the guiding principle of
his government: to reconcile opposing interests in order to
preserve the welfare of country and people. In doing so he had
foresworn the pursuit of honor and had yielded to Haraldr's
legally unfounded claim. In the settlement ceremony he had insisted only on ceremonial rights which symbolically and concretely signified his precedence as king, for instance, his ship
alone is to be anchored in the royal moorage. The difficulty
besetting a personal and governing relationship based principally

on equality, not on precedence, is palpable in Haraldr's challenge to Magnús' right to the royal moorage. Provocatively he anchors his ship in the royal moorage. As Magnús prepares for battle, Haraldr commands his ship to debark. Again an open outbreak of hostilities has been avoided. Yet the fragility of the joint kingship is alluded to in Magnús' summary of the reasons which had led to his aborted attack. Magnús calls Haraldr's provocation an unwarranted test of his authority, a test which inevitably would be followed by other attempts to undermine his power. Haraldr's retort couched in a proverbial saying, that the wiser should yield in a quarrel, only masks his intense anger at having to give way. Snorri singles out expressly this incident as characteristic of the frequent clashes of self-interest between the two rulers. Rather than detailing these incidents he dwells on the role of unwise advisers who invaryingly overplay the dishonor reaped from relinquishing a position in a dispute.[5]

In this chapter Snorri bares the irrationality of conflict engendered by a striving for honor and the invidious strength of societal pressure in sustaining discord. Consequently the chapter serves as a bridge to an understanding of Magnús' self-willed death. A dream, as is usual in *Heimskringla*, reveals the subconscious desires and emotional direction of the dreamer and forecasts the course of his actions. King Óláfr gives Magnús the following choice: a long life-span, unprecedented power, but a life haunted by the commission of a heinous, foolish, and perhaps inexpiable crime, or a short life-span and eternal life in Óláfr's company. When Magnús asks Óláfr to make the choice for him, Óláfr bids his son to follow him.

The heinous crime Magnús would have committed had he decided to live a longer life is the slaying of Haraldr. Implicit in Óláfr's message is also the notion that Haraldr would not have attempted to kill Magnús. That Haraldr's self-control is due to moral constraint rather than affection is clear in the scene following Magnús' death and the many subsequent instances which demonstrate his callousness and vindictiveness in human affairs. Haraldr would not allow human feelings to interfere with the pursuit of power and honor.

Shortly before dying of an illness during a joint campaign against Sveinn, Magnús bequeaths Denmark to Sveinn, presumably because he believed that no Norwegian king other than he himself had the legal and moral right to rule the Danish kingdom. Sveinn, however, was of royal Danish blood and because of his personal qualities commanded his countrymen's affection and loyalty. At Magnús' death Haraldr evinces no sorrow or respect for his nephew's last will. Despite the provisions Magnús had made for his Danish kingdom, Haraldr announces that as heir to Magnús he intends to pursue his claim to Denmark. The answer of Einarr Þambarskelfir, a chieftain who had lived through the reigns of three Norwegian kings, unmasks the flimsiness of Haraldr's claim and his lack of feeling. Einarr replies that he feels more dutybound to take the body of Magnús to its burial ground next to the grave of Saint Óláfr than to fight outside of Norway and to conquer another king's land. The substance of Einarr's speech reveals him as a man who in the course of his long life has achieved spiritual insight. He affirms the principle of conduct which had motivated Magnús to abandon his plans to acquire England: conquest to gratify solely a desire for power is immoral.

As sole ruler of Norway Haraldr appears harsh and relentless in the pursuit of his enemies and persistent in his campaigns against Sveinn. Most of these years are occupied with the persecution of his foes and wars against Denmark. The singleminded cruelty with which Haraldr treats his enemies is seen not only in his entrapments of single chieftains, but also in his merciless treatment of an entire region. His enmities result both from grudge and an inability to tolerate contrary opinions or loyalties conflicting with his interests. He has Einarr Þambarskelfir and his son killed primarily because Einarr, in loyalty to Magnús and Óláfr's legacy, had aborted his campaign against Denmark. Both are slain in an ambush as Einarr, expecting to be reconciled with Haraldr, enters a darkened house. In a similar act of duplicity, he entices Kálfr, a chieftain who had wounded Óláfr at Stiklarstaðir, to return from exile. Ostensibly reconciled, he sends Kálfr and his band of warriors to be slaughtered in battle. The entrapment of Kálfr seems particularly callous as Kálfr's brother, Finnr, Haraldr's most loyal but outspoken chieftain, had exacted the reconciliation as his price for having foiled by diplomacy a revolt against the king.

Haraldr's inability to brook loyalties transcending allegiance to himself is reminiscent of Óláfr's persecution of some chieftains whom he had deemed disloyal. In both cases the allegation is correct only in a narrow sense. The offenders act contrary to the king's interest solely because they are bound to others by such strong personal bonds that the obligation assumes the force of a moral command. The conflict with Hákon Ívarsson arises because of Hákon's obligation toward King Sveinn. Sveinn had spared Hákon's life when Hákon had imprudently brought him the severed head of a marauding nephew. Visibly shaken Sveinn had nevertheless realized that Hákon had merely sought to execute an ambiguous order. Consequently, in an act of gratitude, Hákon rescues Sveinn clandestinely during the rout of Sveinn's fleet in the battle of Niz 1062.

From Haraldr's viewpoint the rescue of Sveinn had been treason, an act aggravated by the universal admiration accorded Hákon for his part in a battle which initially the Norwegians had considered lost. In truth Haraldr had ultimately won the battle himself. He had declared, in the face of Sveinn's overwhelming force, that each of his warriors should fall across each other rather than flee. The escape of Sveinn, however, had cost Haraldr the Danish kingdom he coveted. Yet Haraldr's outrage is motivated not only by his feeling of betrayal but also by jealousy toward Hákon. A measure of Haraldr's animosity is action so swift that in its impulsiveness it seems alien to a man noted for meticulous execution of long-laid plans. As soon as he hears of Sveinn's rescue Haraldr orders his horses to be saddled. Hákon, however, escapes. In a subsequent battle Hákon survives and in a brazen act of daring recaptures his standard, held by one of Haraldr's proven warriors. Realizing that Hákon had eluded him once more Haraldr exclaims in an uncharacteristically impulsive and ineffectual outburst: "The jarl lives. Bring me my armor" (ch. 72, p. 164). The unwitting irony of his words is revealed only later, by Haraldr's inability to rid himself of his enemy. Hákon survives despite Haraldr's formidable reputation as an author of infallible plans.

Haraldr's mercilessness is perhaps best illustrated in his utter disregard for the lives and property of a farming region. In an obvious allusion to Óláfr's refusal to burn Norwegian

villages in his quest to reconquer Norway and to Magnús' magnanimous treatment of his foes, Snorri dwells on Haraldr's acts
of arson by citing brutal evidence from skaldic verses. This
utter disregard of the moral lesson conveyed by Óláfr's conduct
during the battle at Stiklarstaðir underscores Haraldr's cruelty
and signals, together with his quest for self-aggrandizement, the
approach of his defeat and death.

V *The Fall of the Warrior King*

Sveinn's escape from battle had marked a turning point in
Haraldr's fortune. No longer would he be the warrior king whose
ventures would invariably be successful. Thus his long-standing
war with Sveinn would come to an inconclusive end as both kings
swear to uphold peace. Haraldr's failure to conquer Denmark
rankles him, however, and is ultimately responsible for Haraldr's
hapless invasion of England.[6] For the first time in his life
Haraldr listens to self-interested counsel. His famed judgment
had deserted him.

Perhaps it is a sense of not having fulfilled his mission as
warrior king which opens his mind to Tosti, the disgruntled
brother of the Anglo-Saxon king Haraldr Godwineson, who proposed that he should conquer England. Tosti's rationalization of
Haraldr's shortlived objections have the quality of an exernalized
inner voice prodding him to act against his better judgment and
to yield to the dictates of his natural bent. Success had eluded
Haraldr in Denmark, Tosti avers, because he had lacked popular
support, the very reason why Magnús gave up his plan to
invade England. In the proposed conquest of England, however,
Tosti would summon native support. Haraldr's espousal of Tosti's
plan points up the blindness with which he is smitten. On a
secular level he disregards Tosti's self-incriminating statement
that Tosti lacks only his brother's title to be king of England
and he accepts Tosti's assessment that England would be
Haraldr's for the taking. On a spiritual level he is oblivious to
Óláfr's injunction against the conquest of alien lands. That this
transgression will lead to his death is made clear in the ominous
dreams of clairvoyant warriors and in his own dream in which
Óláfr reprimands Haraldr and presages his death in a skaldic

verse. The saint further admonishes Haraldr to follow his example by not seeking combat beyond the confines of his kingdom. The severity of Óláfr's condemnation of Haraldr's planned invasion is evident in a phrase included in the warning verse: "God is not responsible for this" (ch. 82, p. 178). An impulsive and seemingly irrational act prior to the dream discloses as so often is the case an internal struggle to externalize the subconscious. Haraldr after performing the ritual of cutting Óláfr's hair and nails, hurls the key to Óláfr's shrine into the sea. The gesture seems one of despair and suggests an unshakable sense of foreboding.

Interestingly, the initial phase of the invasion is highly successful. Again Haraldr's brilliance as military leader is confirmed. He will suffer defeat only because he is blind to the possibility of treachery. Haraldr is trapped when the townspeople who have sworn him allegiance secretly allow the Anglo-Saxon king to enter the city and advance toward the Norwegian contingent. As Haraldr and his men proceed toward the city, they unsuspectingly go into battle in a holiday mood and, because of the warmth of the day, without the protection of byrnies.[7] Haraldr's death is ultimately occasioned by the instrument of his success. He had conquered by the use of duplicity and he died on account of a well-timed stratagem.

Details of the battle scene at Stamford Bridge reveal his imminent defeat. The inevitability of his death is indicated by the flashing, iced aspect of the advancing army, Haraldr's prefigurative stumble, and his inability to make the right decisions. He refuses to withdraw to his ships to join the rest of his fighting force. He observes unwittingly the Anglo-Saxon king who, pretending to be a royal spokesman, had offered Tosti a third of his kingdom and Haraldr enough land for his grave. Even his spirited combat reminiscent in its ferocity and heedlessness of Magnús' slaughter of the Wends is of no avail. When, under the brunt of Haraldr's savage sword thrusts, his opponents seemingly waver, an arrow shot into Haraldr's mouth kills him. The fierceness of the battle and its hopelessness is indicated in the renewed attacks by the Norwegians. They die as readily as warriors of pagan times who were loath to survive their chieftains in battle. Indeed the ferocity of their attack is a monument

to Haraldr's stature as warrior. His troops would fall one across
the other, even in the absence of his commanding presence.

The *Saga of Haraldr Sigurðarson* ends with a tribute to the
Anglo-Saxon king's magnanimity and with a brief synopsis of
contemporary events in England and Norway. Haraldr Godwineson had allowed the survivors of the battle to depart with
Haraldr's son Óláfr. As Óláfr's brother died of sickness, the survival of the royal house redounds upon this act of generosity. The
saga comes thus to a leisurely and anticlimactic conclusion. There
is the distinct feeling that the age of the giants has passed
and that lesser kings will control the destiny of the realm.

CHAPTER 8

Óláfs saga kyrra,
"Saga of Óláfr the Quiet";
Magnúss saga berfœtts,
"Saga of Magnús the Barelegged"[1]

I *Introduction*

THE sagas on Haraldr's immediate successors, Óláfr the Quiet and Magnús the Barelegged, Óláfr's son, are anticlimactic and in major aspects antithetical. Óláfr's rule was blessed with peace; Magnús' reign stood under the sign of war. The defeat of Haraldr the Hardruler on English soil had a traumatic effect on Óláfr and determined his policy of peaceful development within the land. Óláfr, who, by the magnanimous act of the Anglo-Saxon king, was allowed to return to Norway had no interest in war. In a sense his reign is blessed with the prosperity associated with the peaceful Yngling kings. We hear of buildings being built, of towns being founded by merchants, of court etiquette being elaborated, and of the expansion of royal administration. In a spiritual sense life is occupied with trifling matters and even internal politics, the traditional tensions between kings and peasants, are typified by pettiness rather than by passion. The reign of Magnús, conversely, is filled with imprudent exploits. The peace his father had brought seems to have intensified a bent for violence, the desire to seek redress by retribution, and the search for adventure and excitement abroad.

Despite the obvious difference in character and life-style, the reigns of both kings lack the spiritual fervor and mental achievements of their predecessors. Life is shallow—in Óláfr's reign because there is no conflict or complexity to stimulate

145

greatness; in Magnús' reign because he seeks self-fulfillment only by violence. Of the two kings, Magnús is clearly inferior to his father in stature. Óláfr had the inclination for peace and the willpower and insight to maintain order within the realm. Magnús, in spite of a proven ability to rid the land of Vikings, lacked some of the essential qualities attributed to heroes. He failed to develop or cultivate the generosity expected of kings and which traditionally nurtured loyalty. He also wanted the sound judgment that is indispensable in executing bold ventures.

II   "Saga of Óláfr the Quiet"

Óláfr's reign is singularly uneventful. The impression created is that of a productive though shallow life. Yet a telling episode, essentially a dramatic incident or potentially dramatic situation, encapsulates, as is so often the case in the last third of *Heimskringla,* a more valid judgment on his rule. Óláfr's kingship is a blessing for the land, for he commands respect and provides for the widespread wealth which is engendered only by enduring peace.

The importance of the telling episode in *Óláfs Saga the Quiet* is disclosed in both the subject matter and in the positioning of the scene within the saga. The scene revolves around a traditional point of conflict between king and peasants, the legal duties imposed upon the peasants and the king's implicit right to claim privileges beyond those granted by law. The peasants complain that the king's retinue numbers more men than specified by law. Correspondingly the provisions to be supplied are larger and more burdensome. The king's response is a rebuttal of the implied charge that the enlargement of his retinue represents an abuse of the law and of the peasantry: "I cannot administrate the realm better than I have and I do not inspire more fear than my father did though I have a retinue twice as large as he had. Furthermore I am neither oppressing you for this nor am I making your life more onerous" (ch. 4, p. 207).

The king's retort, the final statement of chapter four in the eight-chapter saga, skillfully contrasts his peaceful administra-

tion with the vindictive cruelty and martial exploits of his
father, Haraldr the Hardruler. The main point is that Óláfr's
peaceful administration has enriched the country. He has
earned his surname, "the Farmer." Óláfr the Farmer (*Óláfr
bóndi*) so benefitted the country that his interests coincided
with those of the peasants. Snorri invalidated the peasants'
complaint in an interesting stylistic manner. The complaint
itself is phrased as a question. There is no explosive confrontation,
only an opportunity to rectify an incorrect interpretation of one
of the king's visible acts. Snorri implies that Óláfr the Quiet or
the Farmer has earned both honorific bynames.

The episode epitomizes the impact of Óláfr's kingship. Despite
the contradictory testimony of a single skaldic verse which
heralds Óláfr as the terror of the English, Snorri only reports
on the peaceful activities of the king: his introduction of a
more elaborate and refined court life, the building of churches
and of a monastery, his support of the guilds, and the establishment of Bergen as a trade center. There is also a comment on
an excess associated with the boredom of peace, boredom relieved
by sartorial extravaganza. Only a poetic epithet which had
become meaningless recalls Óláfr's participation in his father's
ill-fated expedition to England in 1066. Óláfr was the terror
of the English only by virtue of having fought in a successful
battle in his father's hapless campaign.

III   Magnúss saga berfœtts, "Saga of Magnús the Barelegged"

It has often been remarked that Snorri's view of history is
cyclical, that periods of peace will alternate with periods of
war. In contrast to his father's peaceful reign, the rule of
Magnús the Barelegged (1093–1103) stands under the sign of
war, first of civil war, then of expeditions to the British Isles
and Sweden, and finally of adventures in Ireland, where he loses
his life in an ambush. In summarizing Magnús' reign, Snorri
cites a proverb quoted by Magnús himself when his friends
warned him of the danger of waging wars abroad: "A king exists
for glory, not for a long life."[2] The shallowness of this saying
as a motto for life is apparent throughout the saga. The maxim
serves Magnús as a justification for war.

Ironically, the name Magnús ("the Great"), which proved providential for its first royal bearer, Magnús the Good, is attached among his successors to lesser men, kings without vision and enslaved by frailties. *Saga of Magnús the Barelegged* accordingly is filled with examples of Magnús' callousness, his scorn of generosity, and imprudent actions. His first act as king sets the tone of the saga. Ignoring the magnanimous example of his namesake, Magnús the Good, Magnús the Barelegged prepares for war when the Uppland and the Trondheim districts elevate his cousin, Hákon Þórisfóstri, as king over the two regions. He is not prepared to offer Hákon the joint rule over the country, as Magnús the Good had done when Haraldr the Hardruler claimed part of the land.

In the first scenes Snorri adroitly contrasts the character of the two contending kings, suggesting that Hákon would have been the better king. Magnús appears as a man insistent upon maintaining royal privilege and ready to use war to rectify abuse. His encounter with Hákon follows Hákon's unilateral suspension of certain taxes and his conferment of privileges which Magnús rightly believed would lead to the shrinkage of income traditionally enjoyed by kings. The extent of Magnús' anger is seen in the sudden preparation of his warships and in the lighting of immense warning fires on top of the hills. Only the overnight summoning of the region's armed men deters Magnús from attack and forces him to sail precipitously to the South. Hákon, conversely, is characterized as a man of peace and generosity whose goodwill elicits friendship and highmindedness. His entire army, upon being dismissed, promises him friendship and support and accompanies him on a leg of his journey. This portrayal of an able king loved by all and his sudden, untimely death evoke a feeling of ominous futility. Hákon died on a peaceful, pleasurable, but strenuous pursuit. While hunting an elusive ptarmigan, he fell sick and died in the mountains.[3]

Hákon had not begun a civil war. His foster father, Þórir, provokes attack, but he does so out of fear. Snorri clearly states that Þórir, with the support of other chieftains, gathers an opposing army because he realizes that Magnús would not forgive him his role in elevating his foster son, Hákon, as king. A friend of Magnús, however, initiates the hostilities. The

revolt is born, as Magnús' friend summons an army. The subsequent acts of warfare are replete with cruelty and are tinged
with absurdity, as Þórir, crippled by age, must be carried over
the mountains. From beginning to end the revolt is nurtured
by Magnús' inability to redress his wrongs except by violence.
His innate inability to act with generosity and to convey that
he is inclined toward mercy becomes evident in the final
scene of the crushed revolt, the hanging of Þórir and Egill, his
associate. Immobilized by the king's anger, his retainers desist
from pleading for the life of the chieftains. Only after the
hanging of Egill, as the king mutters that Egill in the hour
of need lacked good kinsmen, do they realize that the king had
wished to spare the man's life.

Magnús' conduct of the revolt had unveiled his thoughtless
handling of a manageable crisis. The callousness of Magnús,
however, has still to be confirmed, for his dedication to labor
and his ability to clear the land of Vikings and sea robbers
correct the image of a ruler consumed with anger and vindictiveness. Only in later episodes, subsequent to hapless adventures in Sweden, is there incontrovertible evidence of Magnús' lack of generosity. The episodes involve Skopti, the father
of two of Magnús' closest associates. The conflict of interest
is centered on an inheritance which legally should fall to Skopti.
The arguments forwarded by Skopti and his sons make it clear
that Magnús' insistence on appropriating the inheritance is
illegal. Before the irreparable breach of friendship Skopti reminds the king of his unassailable legal position: he had enough
wits to refrain from disputing with the king a legally unsound
case. Yet he had to act as his ancestors had done before him,
namely to defend a right cause. Two of Skopti's sons, among the
king's most loyal followers, also plead the righteousness of their
cause and recall their sacrifices for him. One had barely escaped
from the Swedes after he had rescued the king from death. The
other had manned a fort which Magnús had foolishly established
on Swedish soil and had suffered the ignominy of defeat. Perhaps
the most incisive phrasing of Magnús' abrogation of his duty to
act with generosity toward his retainers is articulated in a proverb
hurled at the king: "Most people reward the saving of their lives
with evil or with nought" (ch. 19, p. 231). Magnús is clearly not

in the heroic mold. Instead of squandering his fortune in order to reward the loyal comitatus, Magnús deprives his most faithful supporters of their legal property rights.

The correlation of these episodes with Magnús' earlier foolhardy adventure in Sweden displays the dual failing in Magnús' conception of his role as king. A king must be more than a warrior; he must act prudently and generously. In an oblique character-comparison with the Swedish king, the fallacy of Magnús' shallow conception of the kingship becomes apparent. The arrogance that led Magnús to establish an untenable fort in Sweden bespeaks both lack of strategic ability and unconcern for the garrison of three hundred men. The utter defenselessness of the fort is revealed unwittingly in the commander's rejection of an offer of free passage: his men will not be driven like cattle to pasture. They are, however, like sheep penned in. When they finally are forced to sue for peace the Swedish king treats them with magnanimity. Despite their earlier taunts and intransigence they are allowed to depart with only a flogging. Skopti's son points out this act of generosity, alluding to the Swedish king's first offer of free passage to all men and their possessions. He remarks that the Swedish king had acted with the liberality and authority of a great leader. The statement on the Swedish king's liberality implicitly expresses Skopti's contempt for and censure of Magnús as king.

The correlated episodes hence exemplify Magnús' failure as king. The death of Skopti and his sons during their exile on pointless though famous expeditions only underscores the futility and fatuousness of Magnús' conduct. Magnús himself recognizes the consequences of a foolish act only once, at the end of his life during an ambush precipitated by his rash judgment. Observing a baron flee whom he had advanced at the expense of a chieftain he had foolishly outlawed, he subconsciously phrases his own condemnation: *"Óvitr var ek,"* "I was unwise."[4]

In his last battle Magnús exhibits heroically the qualities which distinguished him, the warrior's ability to function under stress and to ignore pain. With both thighs pierced by a spear he seizes the shaft and breaks it between his legs. Fittingly, his surname bespeaks his preoccupation with war for the sake of war. The byname *Styrjaldar-Magnús*, "Battle-Magnús," expresses his fame for having conquered islands off Britain, but likewise condemns him for living solely for the gratification of his passion. Greatness eluded him as he fatuously devalued the content of the heroic motto: "A king shall not think of long life but of fame."

CHAPTER 9

Magnússona saga, "Saga of the Sons of Magnús"; Magnúss saga blinda ok Haralds gilla,[1] "Saga of Magnús the Blind and Haraldr gilli"

I *Introduction*

THE *Saga of Magnús' Sons* presents an interlude between the war-filled years of the previous reign and the violence of the civil war which is to erupt after the death of the last of Magnús' three sons. Again the country seems weary of the levies of battle, as Magnús' three young sons, Sigurðr, Eysteinn, and Óláfr, and their supporters abide by the division of the kingship and the realm. The land is ready for peaceful enterprises mixed with adventure. The major venture in a time span of approximately thirty years is an expedition to the Holy Land and Byzantium during the early years of the reign. Only once is the period of brotherly cooperation broken, by a flare-up of long-concealed jealousy, and then only momentarily. The surviving brothers Eysteinn and Sigurðr are clearly incompatible, each possessing characteristics the other lacks and seemingly disdains. The acrimonious exchange during a social game of comparing stature by vaunting accomplishments is the only fissure allowed to open during the years of joint rule. The difficulties with which this harmony is achieved can be measured only indirectly, by an incident which unveils the passionate nature of Sigurðr, a man noted more for his physical prowess than for his intellect, and later after Eysteinn's death, by Sigurðr's subjection to periodic fits of insanity. Sigurðr's self-control then bears a heroic stamp. He would not violate the bonds
152

of kinship no matter how high the cost. The price would be his acceptance of the inevitable loss of the kingship to his immediate family line. Forwarned by a visionary dream that the realm would slip from the hands of his kin and fall to a newcomer, he accepts unconditionally a hitherto unknown half-brother from Ireland, Haraldr gilli, who proves his paternity by ordeal. As the end of his life approaches he sees the fears of his dream confirmed as his son Magnús treats Haraldr with unrestrained hatred.

The reign of Magnús' sons had been a blessing which was conferred by the rulers' determination to reign in peace. There is passion repressed. Individual cases of cruelty surface. Yet divine grace is manifest. Óláfr's miracles, acts of mercy toward victims of man's bestiality, signal divine approbation of the spiritual and mental quest to preserve and honor brotherly love.

After Sigurðr's death the blessing comes to an abrupt end. The outbreak of civil war, acts of savagery and deceit, are symptomatic of a clash fought solely on a physical plane. Disputes are settled no longer by common agreement but are ended by violent death or inhuman mutilation. The spirit of inhumanity which pervades the entire period of six years is epitomized in the adversities visited upon both kings. Haraldr orders Magnús blinded and mutilated to make him unfit for royal office. Haraldr in turn is stabbed to death in his mistress's bed by a band of men headed by another pretender to the kingship. The saga ends with a communal outburst of moral indignation and with the indication that civil war will continue with the escape of Haraldr's slayer and because of the persistence he demonstrates in pursuing his claim.

II   "Saga of the Sons of Magnús":
The Pressures besetting a Reign of Peace

At Magnús's death his oldest son, Eysteinn, is fifteen, Sigurðr thirteen or fourteen, and Óláfr four or five years of age. The reign of the realm falls temporarily on Eysteinn as Sigurðr and the young chieftains of the land head for an expedition to Byzantium and the Holy Land, lured by accounts of the prodigious wealth in Byzantium and by the prospect of joining the Byzantine emperor's well-paid force. The account of this expedition, with its battles against the pagans of Spain, stopovers in England, France, and

Sicily, and the royal receptions accorded King Sigurðr at Jerusalem and Constantinople comprise more than a third of the saga. The expedition is one of the highpoints in the history of the Norwegian kings. Snorri states that no Norwegians had gone on a more glory-filled journey than King Sigurðr and his men.[2]

The expedition also marks Sigurðr as the warrior king among the brothers and initiates Norway for the first time to ecumenical influence. Given a splinter of the holy cross by Balduin, King of Jerusalem, Sigurðr and twelve of his warriors swear to work for the establishment of an archbishopric in Norway and to establish a tithe.[3] His battles on the way to and in the kingdom of Jerusalem are victorious and his bearing so royal that he is treated at every court with the respect given to the highest dignitaries. In an ahistorical scene Sigurðr is even presented as superior to the Duke of Sicily. While Sigurðr stops over in his duchy, the Duke of Sicily waits on Sigurðr at the table. Sigurðr in turn leads his host to the highseat and confers upon him the kingship over the Sicilian territory. At Jerusalem King Balduin accompanies him to the River Jordan and at Byzantium the emperor offers him the gift of a huge sum of gold or the spectacle of public games. While at Byzantium Sigurðr displays the munificence and the magnificence expected of powerful kings. His ships sail to Byzantium with sails lined with silk. At his arrival the emperor has the imperial gate opened and has silk spread from the gate to the palace. The Norwegians ride to the palace with a sophistication that belied their awe of the imperial wealth and grandeur with which they are greeted. Sigurðr's bearing as the guest of the emperor is that of an equal. He rejects the present of gold in favor of seeing the public games. At his departure he presents the emperor with a munificent gift, all the ships of his fleet, including his own, which is adorned with a gilded figurehead. The present was of such liberality that it occasioned much later a reproach from his brother Eysteinn, as he mocked Sigurðr for having returned to Norway with one ship. That ship, as everyone knew, was not his own but the compassionate gift of the Danish king.

Snorri had described the battles of King Sigurðr on his way to Jerusalem with the disinterest he commonly exhibits toward stock battle scenes. Also, Eysteinn's peaceful building activities during that period receive short shrift. Subsequent chapters, however, clearly demonstrate that despite his admiration for Sigurðr's kingly virtues, King Eysteinn commands his understanding and affection. From the beginning Eysteinn is compared to the best-loved among the Norwegian kings, Hákon the Good and Magnús the Good. In the first chapter on Eysteinn's statesmanship Snorri relates that Eysteinn by acts of friendship extends his power over Jamtaland, a territory that of late had acknowledged the overlord-ship of the Swedish king. The account contains a comparison of Eysteinn to Hákon the Good. Eysteinn himself points out that Jamtaland had given its allegiance to King Hákon. The compari-son, however, runs deeper. Just as King Hákon was treated with affection, King Eysteinn's bid receives unprecedented support. The people of Jamtaland themselves ask him to be their king. The admiration Snorri accords Eysteinn is reflected in the con-cluding sentence of the chapter: "King Eysteinn had conquered Jamtaland with wisdom and not with attacks as some of his an-cestors had done" (ch. 15, p. 256).

A brief eulogy at Eysteinn's death contains the comparison with Magnús the Good: "This is what men said: that over no other man's corpse did so many in Norway stand bereaved since the death of King Magnús, the son of Saint Óláfr the King" (ch. 23, p. 263). The comparison to the good kings of Norway is also sug-gested in the brief characterization of Eysteinn which is found in an entire though short chapter and follows the account of his role in Jamtaland. There is not a single negative noun or adjective in the character portrayal of a king who is temperamentally dis-interested in the glory attained by war.

Nevertheless Snorri provides a corrective, more balanced view of Eysteinn through a traditional saga device, the competitively staged comparison of men of stature during a banquet. Eysteinn himself proposes the game which in saga literature normally re-sults in an outbreak of hostilities. The frivolousness of the pro-posal is evident in Sigurðr's reluctance to participate in a game which depends heavily on verbal skill and which incites hidden or suppressed passion. The vehemence of Sigurðr's subconscious hos-tility toward Eysteinn surges forth in the first charge that as a child Sigurðr was always able to wrestle his older brother to the ground. But the most serious charge in an exchange of accom-plishments and insults is that Eysteinn, though articulate, is considered dishonest. Eysteinn, Sigurðr maintains, speaks to the liking of those who are present. The rebuttal is feeble, reflecting perhaps Snorri's own ambivalence toward an ability shared by artists. Eysteinn has an innate bent to empathize with both parties of a suit. The desire to please all coupled to the necessity of compromise is at the core of the problem.

Sigurðr's passion, his strenuous effort to control it, and his loyalty to Eysteinn are patent in a curious incident which took place prior to the verbal exchange of insults and accomplishments. The incident revolves around a woman, Borghildr, of whom Eysteinn saw a great deal. After Borghildr, disturbed about the gossip, cleared herself by the ordeal of iron, it becomes apparent that Sigurðr had been in love with her.[4] As soon as he hears of Borghildr's vindication, he rides to her father's farm with such vigor that he covers a distance of two days in one. Their son will be the designated and hapless heir, Magnús the Blind. The scene conveys that Sigurðr would not allow even his passion to mar his relationship with Eysteinn.

In both episodes Sigurðr's self-control is a measure of his commitment to honor the duty of brotherly love. How difficult it is for him to achieve this self-mastery becomes evident only in later scenes, for these indicate that the intensity of his passion may have been a mild manifestation of the mental illness which befalls him after Eysteinn's death. The illness is described in an understated manner as lack of calmness and restlessness of mind. Fits of uncontrollable laughter and an occasional outburst of cruelty unrelated to the offense suggest the presence of periodic insanity. That this uncontrollable desire to inflict cruel punishment may have been an inherited burden is indicated by a miracle performed by Saint Óláfr on a hapless and poor young man. Sigurðr's mother had his tongue cut out for a trivial offense. The youth had partaken of some food from her platter.[5] This uncontrollable temper, unmitigated by the wisdom of Sigurðr, will also be a dominant character trait of his son Magnús. The propensity for and occasional indulgence of violence and passion foreshadow the dissolution of goodwill among later contestants for the kingship.

The control Sigurðr exercises over his passion, his sense of fair play and loyalty, inspire the trust and affection of his people which Sigurðr, despite his bouts of insanity, commanded. He is also credited with wisdom so deep that it manifests itself in mystic insight. In a dream so perturbing that upon his awakening his men scarcely dare approach him, he foresees the diminishing stature of future kings and the loss of the kingship to his immediate kin. He perceives a black cloud in the sea drifting toward land and recognizes a large tree with its roots in the water. As the tree hits the shore it breaks into pieces which float into every bay of the country. Most of the pieces are small, though some are larger. The tree, as Sigurðr recognizes, is the mystic image of a man who will make his home in Norway and whose offspring will spread over the country.[6]

Sigurðr's pessimistic vision contrasts strangely with the parallel dreams of Hálfdan the Black and Ragnhildr, his queen. The progenitors of the historic kings of Norway foresaw the flowering of their family line. Sigurðr, the father of Magnús, the future king who is to be deposed, maimed, castrated, and blinded, is shocked by a vision portending doom. As the dream partially fulfills itself during the last years of Sigurðr's reign, Sigurðr displays the fairness and firmness of character that inspire respect and awe. When a man from Ireland arrives contending that he is the son of Magnús the Barelegged, Sigurðr's father, Sigurðr bids him prove his descent by an ordeal. The man, Gillikristr, known later as Haraldr, consents to walk on nine glowing plowshares and passes the ordeal. Henceforth Sigurðr would not allow Haraldr to be harmed. He would not try to counter the gloomy events he had envisioned. Sigurðr's resolve to act righteously toward a brother un-Norwegian in speech, manners, and physical skills is amply demonstrated. He will not allow his son Magnús to make a fool of Haraldr, and when Haraldr, engaged in a brawl, is about to be hanged, he rescues him with impulsive dispatch. The scene leading to the rescue of Haraldr is one of the highpoints of the saga. Sigurðr, in deep sleep, is awakened by a chieftain whom irrationally he has forbidden to come into his sight. The chieftain sternly reminds him of the business at hand: his duty to help his brother. Sigurðr's gratitude toward a man he had hated is revealed in simple, heartfelt words: "Never do I want to be without you" (ch. 29, p. 271).

With the passing of years Sigurðr ironically begins to resemble his brother, if not in agility of mind, then in the performance of

his kingly duties. The warrior king conducts only one war, a war
not initiated by himself but by the Danish king. He is a builder
and fortifier of towns. He also elicits affection to the extent that
all districts in the realm swear that after his death Magnús will
be king. This is the major provision he makes to support the succession of his son. The saga, however, ends on a pessimistic note
with the flare-up of unbridgeable tensions between Magnús and
Haraldr.

This scene revolves around a contest, not a verbal comparison
of skills as with Eysteinn and Sigurðr, but a demonstration of
physical speed. Even in the race, a mere competition of skills,
Magnús' arrant arrogance toward Haraldr is evident to all. Despite the provocations and the unjust handicaps imposed upon
him, Haraldr remains courteous. As winner of the game he shows
no rancor. Sigurðr, however, rebukes Magnús. In a speech censuring Magnús' immature ways, he compares his own son to a foolish
colt. His powerlessness to guide the conduct of Magnús after his
death and to prevent his fate is subconsciously expressed in the
last sentence of his reprimand: "Don't you ever again make a fool
of him [Haraldr] while I am alive" (ch. 27, p. 268).

The physical nature of the contest between Magnús and
Haraldr subtly indicates the contestants' mental and spiritual in-
feriority to Eysteinn and Sigurðr. Both Magnús and Haraldr will
react on a physical plane in their bitter dispute over the succession. Neither will have the mental and spiritual resources to settle their quarrels for the sake of their kinship and the welfare of
their realm. The foolish quarrelsomeness had emerged once in
Sigurðr's and Eysteinn's reign during their verbal game comparing
their statures and accomplishments. The verbal game which
usually results in hostilities and bloodshed is but an outburst of
tensions inherent in the sharing of power by equals. The physical
contest between Magnús and Haraldr, conversely, serves to expose Magnús' abiding animosity toward Haraldr and presages
the irreparable and foolish rupture between the two kinsmen.
Sigurðr's self-discipline, his mastery of his jealousy toward Eysteinn, is a mark of his personal stature and enables him to complete a reign that is a blessing to his people. Snorri emphasizes
this blessing by placing this assessment at the conclusion of the
saga. As with the peaceful Yngling kings of the prehistoric era,

Sigurðr's rule provides his people both with *ár ok friðr*, "fertility and peace" (ch. 33, p. 277).

III   "Saga of Magnús the Blind and Haraldr gilli," *The Witless Destruction of the Kingship's Ethical Base*

The pessimism which had pervaded the last part of the *Saga of Magnús' Sons* permeates the saga of his successors. Significantly, the saga lacks even a single account of a miracle performed by Óláfr. The implication is that not even a miracle brings a ray of hope into a pitiless world.

The first chapter is an exposé of the labile political affairs after Sigurðr's death. At the outset of the chapter Snorri provides a verbal characterization of the opponents in order to emphasize that the lack of royal character, the loosening of moral inhibitions, and the concomitant loss of ethical will effect the senseless acts of cruelty which characterize the era. The position of the traditional summary characterizations in the saga is unusual. This departure from common practice focuses attention on and foreshadows the internecine dissension which will lead ineluctably to the violent death of both contestants. The characteristics attached to Magnús bode ill for the future of the country. A king who is stingy, grim, and hostile in manner will be unable to command the loyalty of his men. Indeed, the initial support given to Magnús is predicated upon his father's popularity and the respect given to Sigurðr. Magnús will inevitably fail as his father's friends abandon him. Conversely, Haraldr's easygoing charm and his willingness to allow others to act on his behalf win him the allegiance of chieftains.

All details which follow the verbal characterizations contribute to the aura of gloom. The agreement stipulating a joint kingship represents solely an uneasy truce. The fragility of the pact is intimated by an almost disinterested factual account of Magnús' dissatisfaction. In addition, Magnús' friendly relations with the Danish king come to an unfortunate end. In a foolish move Magnús rejects his wife, the sister of the Danish king, and has her sent back to Denmark. Consequently, Magnús would be deprived of the ready source of support from a power that had traditionally and self-seekingly backed ventures on Norwegian soil.[7]

The hostilities between Magnús and Haraldr break out four years after the political settlement. At first the skirmishes are of minor political consequence. They are characterized, however, by lack of compassion toward the peasantry. The unthinking cruelty toward the peasants indulged in by both parties is highlighted in an episode which is paradigmatic of the chain of merciless and senseless acts which are to follow. The episode takes place on the battlefield, in the first major confrontation between Magnús and Haraldr. Haraldr's half-brother, a warrior acknowledged as a leader of the battle, is killed from behind. His slayer is a peasant, a victim of the war, who after suffering the wanton destruction of his farm and induction into Haraldr's army, had waited for the moment of revenge. The incident commands more than passing interest. Snorri, in a manner similar to that of his nephew Sturla in *Íslendinga saga,* suggests that cruelty will engender cruelty in a chain of events broken only occasionally by acts of loyalty, love, and compassion.

Haraldr had lost this battle, but the defeat ironically also marked the turning point in his fortunes. Unexpectedly, the large number of troops that Magnús had rallied to his cause evaporated. Magnús, in the foolish hope that Haraldr had been beaten decisively, or fancying that the army could be summoned hastily, had dismissed his troops. The foolishness of this act is underscored by the fact that he acted alone against the seasoned counsel of his advisers.

That foolishness will deprive him of the realm and lead to his mutilation is revealed in an anecdotal scene between him and Sigurðr, the councillor most trusted by his father, Sigurðr. As in the previous saga Magnús' foolishness is defined as lack of maturity or character. He will reject Sigurðr's advice three times. Magnús is not wise enough to offer half of the kingship to Haraldr who had invaded Norway with troops from Denmark and had won support in the land. He is not cruel enough to have those chieftains killed who are withdrawing their support, and he is not independent enough to forego his pride momentarily and flee to the northernmost district, to the regional cornerstone of his power. The scene ends in gloom. Sigurðr's departure, his abandonment of Magnús, will signal the end of Magnús' rule and of a life of dignity.

Sigurðr Sigurðarson represents not only a traditional warning-figure but also a protective figure. By a peculiar circumstance he is the namesake of Magnús' father. In addition he bears the same name in his patronymic. The bearing of the same name suggests similarity in character. Indeed, the scenes in which Sigurðr is associated with Sigurðr the King reveal the strength of character and convictions common to both. The difference in the men's character redounds partly on difference in function. Sigurðr, the loyal retainer of Sigurðr the King, will enable the king to live up to his moral commitments. As a warning-figure Sigurðr Sigurðarson verbalizes and supports the king's moral precepts. Conversely, Sigurðr had futilely given Magnús three harsh choices to uphold his rule. When Sigurðr withdrew from Magnús' council of chieftains, he left with the prophecy that Magnús would suffer either death or shame. Sigurðr's departure signifies, then, on a realistic and spiritual level the hopelessness of Magnús' self-made fate.

Haraldr's return to Norway is marked by a politic mixture of conciliatoriness and cruelty. In effect Haraldr implements the policies implicit in Sigurðr's counsel to Magnús. Haraldr is conciliatory to those who wish to be his friends and merciless to his enemies. As he nears land he sends a delegation to plead his case to the assembled peasant army. The peasant army disbands, believing that Haraldr wishes to acquire only what is his due. Haraldr's innate cruelty is unleashed against Magnús' staunch supporters. Snorri cites the death meted out to two chieftains who were Magnús' friends. One suffered death by hanging, the other by being hurled into a waterfall. The choice of death had been made by the first chieftain, the other had to submit to the second form of execution. The recital of Haraldr's cruelty is clearly prefigurative. It foreshadows the dismal fate of Magnús, who upon capture is blinded, castrated, and maimed. The reason for this act of cruelty is the unfounded hope that Magnús would no longer be called king.

Haraldr's disinclination to engage in battle is a curious character trait in a man noted for signal acts of atrocity. This unwillingness to expose himself to the dangers of war seems to have been innate, as Snorri indicates by quoting Haraldr's fainthearted response prior to the first battle he was forced to

fight with Magnús. Upon hearing that Magnús' superior army is
approaching his camp Haraldr exclaims with ingenuous disbelief:
"What could my kinsman King Magnús want? It could not be
that he wishes to do battle with us?" (ch. 2, p. 280). Once he
had defeated Magnús, this unpreparedness to do combat combined with the unresolved tensions within the realm have serious
consequences. Norway is open to invasion by a huge Wendish
fleet which destroys the city of Konungahella and takes many
of its citizens as prisoners. The desolation wrought by the
Wendish army is patent in two remarks: the city was never
rebuilt to its former glory and the inhabitants who were ran-
somed never achieved the stature and prosperity they had
enjoyed before the invasion. The abrogation of Haraldr's responsibility in defending the country against the perils of the
Wends is evident in one sentence only, the warning sent to the
city by the Danish King Eiríkr and Archbishop Ozurr. Haraldr is
either unable to assess the danger or unprepared to ward it off.

The immediate cause of Haraldr's death is his inability to
reconcile the aristocratic faction which is clandestinely loyal
to Magnús. Correlated to the dissension bred by conflicting
loyalties is the use of deceit by both parties. Again Snorri
shows how deceit leads to deceit, corroding the moral fiber of
society, its prime source of strength. The end of Haraldr's rule
is signaled by the appearance of another hitherto unknown
pretender to the throne, Sigurðr slembidjákn, whose declaration
that he had proven himself to be the son of Magnús the Barelegged by an ordeal taken in Denmark indicates the possibility
of deceit. The questionability of this ordeal is intimated by
its provenance in a country which had a historical interest in
fomenting discord in Norway. The manner in which Sigurðr
slembidjákn had submitted to the ordeal contrasts hence sharply
with Haraldr gilli's own proof of his paternity. Haraldr's ordeal
had been supervised by the Norwegian bishop and witnessed by
the Norwegian court. Haraldr's reception of Sigurðr slembidjákn,
his supposed half-brother, is also markedly different from the
circumspect but honest reception given him by King Sigurðr.
Haraldr received Sigurðr slembidjákn with guile and ill-concealed
hate inspired by Sigurðr slembidjákn's participation in the slaying
of a good friend.

During King Sigurðr's reign Haraldr had been vouchsafed an honored existence protected against his enemies, including Sigurðr's own son. For King Sigurðr the ties of blood were too sacred to be violated. Haraldr tacitly rejects Sigurðr slembidjákn's claim to kinship and recognizes no moral constraint toward the pretender. In a move which seems inspired as much by fear of Sigurðr slembidjákn as by the urge for blood revenge, Haraldr and his chieftains plot Sigurðr's death. Only Sigurðr's presence of mind, his daring, and his physical stamina account for his survival in a well-planned but poorly executed scheme.

The treachery with which Haraldr gilli had treated Sigurðr slembidjákn has become part of life at court. Magnús' followers, now retainers of Haraldr, await the opportune moment for betraying Haraldr. Two of these, by discovering through jest that Haraldr is to sleep with his mistress rather than with the queen, provide Sigurðr slembidjákn with the opportunity to kill the king. As Haraldr is sleeping stuporously drunk next to his mistress, Sigurðr and his men burst into the sparsely guarded room and slay him. The brutality of the act is emphasized not by the first assault but by the subsequent synchronous stabbing of the intoxicated king.

The monstrosity of the act is again illustrated in a public scene and in the commitment of the chieftains to maintain peace during their lifetime between Haraldr gilli's sons. The public scene follows the slaying of Haraldr gilli. Sigurðr slembidjákn and his supporters row to the bridge in Bergen where Sigurðr announces the killing and asks for recognition as king. The moral shock over the disclosure bursts forth in a communal rejection of Sigurðr's demand. They all answer "as if with one mouth" that they would never obey or serve a man who had murdered his brother and "if he was not your brother, you do not have the ancestral right to be king" (ch. 6, p. 301). The scene ends with the outlawing of Sigurðr and his companions.

The saga does not conclude with this expression of moral outrage. Instead the saga ends on a realistic note. The peasants in two districts accept Sigurðr as king on the local things. This bare fact briefly told points to major events in the next saga, the hardships of the civil war which will ensue as Sigurðr doggedly pursues his claim to the realm.

CHAPTER 10

Conclusion:
"The Saga of Haraldr's Sons," "The Saga of Hákon the Broadshouldered," "The Saga of Magnús Erlingsson"[1]

S NORRI concludes *Heimskringla* with a deepening sense of pessimism which in the last saga of the series reaches its nadir. The feeling of gloom inspires the unifying themes of the three sagas, the elusiveness of peace and the concomitant loosening of moral and societal bonds. Civil war threatens the legitimate rule of Haraldr gilli's sons at the beginning of their saga. Civil war erupts again toward the end of the saga and continues unabated in the time span covered by the final two sagas. Only once is there a sustained period of peace. During those sixteen years the regents of the royal infants impose a peace which would collapse with the advent of their death. Two of Haraldr gilli's sons would renew the civil war in a mindless quest for greater power.[2]

The civil war which had rent the realm during the early reign of Haraldr gilli's sons had manifested a dangerous loosening of self-restraint among the claimants to the rule. Most prominent is the unscrupulous campaign of Magnús the Blind to regain the kingdom. Despite his debilitating mutilation Magnús, released by a pretender from monastic confinement, vows a relentless war. His deceitful recruitment of foreign troops to fight for his cause discloses a total disregard of the realm he claims as his own. This selfish pursuit of private goals reemerges after the regents' death. Two of Haraldr gilli's sons, Sigurðr and Eysteinn, plot their brother Ingi's death. Ingi's deformity and physical weakness, they avow, render him unfit for office. This and the mindless indulgence of character frailties

164

underscore their obliviousness to the lesson of brotherhood conveyed by the death of Magnús the Good. Magnús the Good had willed his death, for he wanted to avoid killing Haraldr the Hardruler in a fit of passion, whereas Eysteinn and Sigurðr callously scheme the deposition of their able and kindhearted brother.

This mindlessness is shown to be part of the social fabric flawing even outstanding members of political life. For the first time we encounter in Grégóríús Dagsson, a beloved and treasured friend of King Ingi, a form of heroism which, though glorious, is vitiated by rash judgment. Even the intellect formerly esteemed as the font of wisdom is misused in the implacable drive for power. Erlingr, Ingi's *de facto* successor, hones his intellect into a brilliant and many-faceted weapon of destruction. During his rule as regent for his son Magnús, Erlingr would relentlessly destroy his declared and suspected enemies. At the end of the saga Magnús appears in the partial image of his father slaughtering an opposing army as if it were a herd of defenseless cattle. Snorri had remarked that Erlingr's grimness had spawned much of the unrest which had beset the country. Thus Magnús' remorseless killing of a defeated army, together with omens of Erlingr's approaching death, point to yet another period of civil war to be waged by the remnant of the routed insurgents. Erlingr's policy of mercilessness had not produced the stability he had hoped to achieve. The brilliance of his mind had served only to stave off the self-perpetuated threat of defeat, but had failed to bring permanent peace. *Heimskringla* ends accordingly on a gloomy, inconclusive note. The civil war will continue because Saint Óláfr's spiritual legacy, the obligation to preserve the peace and integrity of the realm, has fallen into oblivion.

Notes and References

Chapter One

1. Only one poem, "Háttatal," dedicated to Jarl Skúli (1217–1240) and King Hákon Hákonarson (1217–1263) is extant. Of another poem honoring Jarl Skúli a refrain susceptible to parody survived.
2. "Prologus," *Heimskringla I*, p. 5. Snorri singles out those poems which poets composed for and recited publicly to contemporary rulers and their courts.
3. In *Heimskringla* alone Snorri rescued from oblivion 613 stanzas.
4. Jakob Benediktsson, "Hvar var Snorri nefndur höfundur Heimskringlu?," *Skírnir*, 129 (1955), 118–27, suggests that a manuscript still extant in the sixteenth century named Snorri as the author of *Heimskringla*.
5. See the edition by Sigurður Nordal (Reykjavík, 1933), pp. lxx–xcv, and among modern contributions the controversial studies by Peter Hallberg, *Snorri Sturluson og Egils saga Skallagrímssonar, ett försök till språklig författarbestämming*, Studia Islandica Nr. 20 (Reykjavík, 1962); *Stilsignalement och författarskap i norrön saga-litteratur, synpunkter och exempel*, Acta Universitatis Gothoburgensis, Nordistica Gothoburgensia Nr. 3 (Göteborg, 1968), pp. 7–51.
6. The authoritative work on Snorri Sturluson's life is Sigurður Nordal, *Snorri Sturluson* (1920; repr. Helgafell, 1972). See also his review article, "Snorri Sturluson, nokkurar hugleiðingar á 700. ártíð hans," *Skírnir*, 115 (1941), pp. 5–33; Fredrik Paasche, *Snorre Sturlason og Sturlungene*, 2nd ed. (Oslo, 1948); Gunnar Benediktsson, *Snorri, skáld í Reykholti* (Reykjavík, 1957), and *Ísland hefur jarl. Nokkrir örlagaþættir Sturlungaaldar* (Reykjavík, 1954), pp. 23–44.
7. *Íslendinga saga*, available to me in the edition by Guðni Jónsson, *Sturlunga saga II* (Reykjavík, 1954).
8. Sturla Þórðarson authored *Hákonar saga Hákonarsonar* and *Magnúss saga lagabœtis* and is credited with an important version of *Landnámabók*, "Book of Settlements." He may have authored two additional sagas. See *Sturlu þáttr*, ch. 2, pp. 375–79, for an account of his literary versatility and charm as a storyteller.
9. Transl. Julia H. McGrew, in *Sturlunga Saga* (New York, 1970), I, ch. 136, p. 333, referred to hereafter only by chapter and page.

For an interesting description of the era, see Einar Ól. Sveinsson, *The Age of the Sturlungs: Icelandic Civilization in the Thirteenth Century,* trans. Jóhann S. Hannesson, Islandica Nr. 36 (Ithaca, 1953); Haraldur Bessason, trans., *A History of the Old Icelandic Commonwealth: Íslendinga saga by Jón Jóhannesson,* University of Manitoba Icelandic Studies, Nr. 2 (Manitoba, 1974), pp. 222–82.

10. See *Sturlu saga,* pp. 103–82, for a description of Sturla and his pursuit of power; also Peter G. Foote, "Sturlusaga and its Background," *Viking Society for Northern Research, Saga-Book,* 13, Pt. 4 (1950–51), particularly pp. 222–37; W. H. Vogt, "Charakteristiken aus der Sturlungasaga, A. Sturlusaga," *Zeitschrift für deutsches Altertum,* 54 (1913), pp. 376–95.

11. See *Oddaverja þáttr,* in *Þorláks saga, Þorláks saga in yngri,* ch. 2, pp. 136–37.

12. See Halldór Hermannsson, *Sæmund Sigfússon and the Oddaverjar,* Islandica, Nr. 22 (Ithaca, 1932); Einar Ól. Sveinsson, *Sagnaritun Oddaverja,* Studia Islandica, Nr. 1 (Reykjavík, 1937).

13. *Jóns saga helga,* chs. 15–16, pp. 22–24; Helen T. McM. Buckhurst, "Sæmundr inn fróði in Icelandic Folklore," *Viking Society for Northern Research, Saga-Book,* 11 (1928–36), pp. 84–92.

14. *Páls saga byskups,* ch. 1, pp. 253–54; Anne Holtsmark, *En islandsk scholasticus fra det 12 århundre,* Det Norske Videnskaps-Akademi i Oslo, hist.-filos. klasse (Oslo, 1936).

15. *Páls saga byskups,* ch. 9, pp. 265–66; *Hungrvaka,* ch. 10, p. 27; "Um stafrofit," *Edda Snorra Sturlusonar,* II, p. 12.

16. For accounts attributable to Jón, see *Magnúss saga Erlingssonar,* ch. 21, p. 395 and *Mangúss saga blinda ok Haralds gilla,* chs. 9–12, pp. 288–96, in *Heimskringla III.* On Ari's stature, see "Prologus," *Heimskringla I,* particularly pp. 5–6.

17. Ed. Finnur Jónsson, *Den norsk-islandske skjaldedigtning* (København: Gyldendalske boghandel, 1912), I, B, pp. 575–90.

18. Ed. Einar Ól. Sveinsson, Matthías Þórðarson, *Íslensk fornrit* Nr. 4, ch. 65, pp. 183–84.

19. See *Ættartölur,* ch. 2, p. 81; *Íslendinga saga,* chs. 16, 53, pp. 23, 128.

20. *Sturlu saga,* chs. 34, 31, pp. 180, 174–75 respectively.

21. See *Íslendinga saga,* ch. 26, p. 46; *Þættir úr miðsögu Guðmundar byskups,* ch. 9, p. 414; *Guðmundar saga Ararsonar eftir Arngrím ábóta,* ch. 47, p. 301, for the addressees of the archiepiscopal letter.

22. *Íslendinga saga,* chs. 35, 38, pp. 73–74, 83–85, and *Hákonar saga Hákonarsonar,* ch. 56, p. 503. See Jón Jóhannesson, *Íslendinga saga II, Fyrirlestrar og ritgerðir um tímabilið 1262–1550* (no pl. pub.:

Notes and References

Almenna bókafélagið, 1958, pp. 210–211, for Snorri's *lendr-maðr* status, a unique distinction for an Icelander.

23. "Oddaveria Annall (L) 1238–1248," *Islandske Annaler indtil 1578*, ed. Gustav Storm (Christiania, 1888), p. 481; Nils Hallan, "Snorri fólgsnarjarl," *Skírnir*, 146 (1972), pp. 159–76, discusses Hákon's legal justification in seeking Snorri's death and the subsequent claims on Snorri's property.

Chapter Two

1. Dag Strömbäck, "The Dawn of West Norse Literature," in *Bibliography of Old Norse-Icelandic Studies 1963* (Copenhagen, 1964); G. Turville-Petre, *Origins of Icelandic Literature* (Oxford, 1953); Hans Bekker-Nielsen, Thorkil Damsgaard Olsen, Ole Widding, *Norrøn Fortællekunst, Kapitler af den norsk-islandske middelalder-litteraturs historie* (Copenhagen, 1965). For the chronology of manuscripts, extant manuscripts, editions, and scholarly literature, see Kurt Schier, *Sagaliteratur* (Stuttgart, 1970).

2. See *First Grammatical Treatise, the Earliest Germanic Phonology*, ed., trans. Einar Haugen, Language Monograph Nr. 25, Supplement to *Language*, 26 (1950), pp. 12–13: "I have composed an alphabet for us Icelanders as well, in order that it might be made easier to write and read, as is now customary in this country as well, the laws, the genealogies, the sacred writings, and also that historical lore which Ari Thorgilsson has recorded in his books with such understanding wit."

3. See the opening sentence of *First Grammatical Treatise*, p. 12: "In most countries men chronicle in books the great events that have come to pass within their country . . . ," and the sentiment expressed in *Saxonis Gesta Danorum*, I, Bk. I, 1, p. 3.

4. Sigurður Nordal, *Sagalitteraturen*, in *Litteraturhistorie B. Norge og Island* (Stockholm, 1953), pp. 195–97; Turville-Petre, *Origins of Icelandic Literature*, p. 169. See respectively *First Grammatical Treatise*, p. 13, and *Haraldssonar saga*, *Heimskringla III*, ch. 11, p. 319, for judgments on Ari and Eiríkr.

5. See, for instance, the episode in *Íslendings þáttr sögufróða*, in *Íslendinga þættir*, pp. 148–50.

6. The dates are taken from *Origins of Icelandic Literature*.

7. Turville-Petre, *Origins of Icelandic Literature*, pp. 175–96. Oddr Snorrason's *Saga Óláfs Tryggvasonar*, contains, however, also heroic matter and lively, popular tales.

8. The tale is about Snæfríðr, a beautiful sorceress from Lappland (*Ágrip*, chs. 3–4, pp. 3–5).

Chapter Three

1. For references, see Finnur Jónsson's edition, *Edda Snorra Sturlusonar*. For an introduction and bibliography, see Anne Holtsmark, "Edda, den yngre," *Kulturhistorisk leksikon for nordisk middelalder* (København, 1958), III, 475–480. The title *Edda* might refer to the farm Oddi or to the Old Norse work for poetry, *'óðr.'*

2. A kenning is a poetic circumlocution consisting of at least two nouns; e.g., Þórr is called the son of Óðinn.

3. Most studies treat the mythological and religious content of the work, the authenticity of the mythological matter, the intrusion of Christian thought into pagan myths, and the problem of the prologue, in which the Æsir are Trojans from Asia who assume divinity by virtue of fraud. Anne Holtsmark, *Studier i Snorres mytologi*, Det Norske Videnskaps-Akademi i Oslo, Skrifter, II. hist.-filos. klasse, ny serie Nr. 4 (Oslo, 1964) shows that Snorri was conversant with ecclesiastical idiom and that his style reveals a thorough scholastic training. Siegfried Beyschlag, "Die Betörung Gylfis," *Zeitschrift für deutsches Altertum*, 85 (1954), pp. 163–81, is primarily concerned with the beguiling of Gylfi's mind. See also Hans Kuhn, "Das nordgermanische Heidentum in den ersten christlichen Jahrhunderten," *Zeitschrift für deutsches Altertum*, 79 (1942–43), pp. 133–66; Anker Teilgård Laugesen, "Snorres opfattelse af Aserne," *"Arkiv för nordisk filologi*, 57 (1942), pp. 301–15. For the viewpoint that Snorri's mythological material is inauthentic, see Eugen Mogk, *Zur Bewertung der Snorra-Edda als religionsgeschichtliche und mythologische Quelle des nordgermanischen Heidentums* (Leipzig, 1932) and Walter Baetke, *Die Götterlehre der Snorra-Edda* (Berlin, 1952), issued respectively as Berichte über die Verhandlungen der Sächsischen Akademie der Wissenschaften zu Leipzig, Phil.-hist. Klasse, Nrs. 84 and 97.

4. The translations are mine unless otherwise noted.

5. Transl. Jean I. Young, *The Prose Edda of Snorri Sturluson, Tales from Norse Mythology*, p. 52.

6. See Sigurður Nordal's interpretation of "Völuspá," in "Three Essays on Völuspá," *Viking Society for Northern Research, Saga Book*, 18 (1970–73), pp. 79–135.

7. *Heiti* is a poetic substitute.

8. See Andreas Heusler, *Die gelehrte Urgeschichte im altisländischen Schrifttum*, Abhandlungen der preussischen Akademie der Wissenschaften in Berlin, Hist.-phil. Kl. (Berlin, 1908). Kees W. Bolle, "In Defense of Euhemerus," *Myth and Law among the Indo-Europeans*, ed. Jaan Puhwel (Berkeley, 1970), pp. 29–30, points out

that Snorri's thinking is deeply mythical. When Snorri localizes Troy in Turkey near the center of the earth, he could not have phrased it "more mythologically," since the gods always live near the center of the earth.

9. See Konstantin Reichardt, "Die Thórsdrápa des Eilífr Goðrúnarson: Textinterpretation," *PMLA*, 63 (1948), pp. 329–91.

10. "Háttalykill" (ca. 1145), ed. Jón Helgason, Anne Holtsmark, *Háttalykill enn forni*, Bibliotheca Arnamagnæana Nr. 1.

Chapter Four

1. Gustav Storm, ed., *Monumenta historica Norvegiæ*, pp. 69–124.

2. *Hákonarssaga Hákonarson*, ch. 285, p. 624.

3. Snorri's *Óláfs saga helga* exists also as a separate work and is referred to as such. It also exists in interpolated versions. See Sigurður Nordal, *Om Olaf den helliges saga, en kritisk undersøgelse* (København, 1914).

4. See Siegfried Beyschlag, "Möglichkeiten mündlicher Überlieferung in der Königssaga," *Arkiv för nordisk filologi*, 68 (1953), pp. 109–39.

5. The only version of the saga that Snorri surely knew was written ca. 1220 by Styrmir the Wise. Styrmir's work is lost except for fragments in *Flateyjarbók* and other reworkings of Snorri's "Saga of Óláfr the Saint." It is doubtful or unknown whether he knew other versions.

6. For a discussion on the prehistoric Yngling kings, see Marlene Ciklamini, "Ynglinga saga: Its Function and Its Appeal," *Mediaeval Scandinavia*, 8 (1975), pp. 86–99.

7. *Heimskringla I*, pp. 94–149. The dating of Haraldr's life is controversial as is the dating of the lives of his immediate successors. For a thorough discussion of chronological problems, see Ólafía Einarsdóttir, *Studier i kronologisk metode i tidlig islandsk historieskrivning* (Lund, 1964).

8. Ed. P. A. Munch, pp. 3–13. For Fagrskinna's dating, see Bjarni Aðalbjarnarson, *Om de norske kongers sagaer*, Det Norske Videnskaps-Akademi i Oslo, Skrifter II, hist.-filos. kl. (Oslo, 1936), p. 176.

9. In *Heimskringla* Haraldr never sought to extend his dominion beyond the confines of Norway. He only sought to defend his land from within and without against ravaging Vikings.

10. Allodium is old inherited land to which the king had no legal right. The allodium question revolves around the type of tax imposed. The tax is thought of as a realty or a head tax.

172 SNORRI STURLUSON

11. The emigrants are Haraldr's unrelenting enemies. Also the colonization of Iceland and of the Faroe Islands is related to the wars waged during the unification.

12. Ch. 43, p. 149. *Fagrskinna*, p. 14.

13. This is a proverbial saying. Hákon's role as a lawgiver and his respect for law contribute to his greatness.

14. *Heimskringla I*, pp. 198–224 (ruled from 961–970).

15. *Heimskringla I*, pp. 225–372.

16. Toralf Berntsen, "Sagaringen om Olav Trygvason," *Edda*, 22 (1924), p. 227. See also Motifs H311, T55, in Stith Thompson, *Motif-Index of Folkliterature* (Bloomington, Indiana, 1956, 1957), III, p. 398, V, p. 340; Inger M. Boberg, *Motif-Index of Early Icelandic Literature*, Bibliotheca Arnamagnæana Nr. 27 (Copenhagen, 1966), pp. 151, 243.

17. Gwyn Jones, "The Historian and the Jarl," *History Today*, 19 (1969), p. 235. Lars Lönnroth, "Studier i Olaf Tryggvasons saga," *Samlaren*, 84 (1963), pp. 54–94, treats the fictional character of the entire tradition; Gwyn Jones, *The Legendary History of Olaf Tryggvason* (Glasgow, 1968).

18. The episode is modeled on a dialogue of Pope Gregory, in which Saint Benedict and the Gothic King Totila are the actors. For the dialogue in Old Norse, see Þorvaldur Bjarnarson, ed., *Leifar fornra kristinna frœða íslenzkra*, pp. 147–48.

19. See also a doublet to the story, ch. 78, p. 325.

20. The term of abuse connoted an emotive abrogation of Jarl Hákon's legal standing and loss of personal honor. Óláfr ruled from 995–1000.

Chapter Five

1. For the literary aspects of the saga, see in particular Fredrik Paasche, "Heimskringlas Olavssaga: Komposition, stil, karaktertegning," *Edda*, 6 (1916), pp. 365–83; Hallvard Lie, *Studier i Heimskringlas stil: Dialogene og talene*, Det Norske Videnskaps-Akademi i Oslo, Skrifter, II, hist.-filos. kl. (Oslo, 1937 [for 1936]). Anthony Faulkes, *Rauðúlfs Þáttr, A Study*, Studia Islandica, Nr. 21 (Reykjavík, 1966).

2. Hans Kjær, "St. Canute and St. Olaf in the Church of the Nativity, Bethlehem," *Viking Society for Northern Research, Saga Book*, 11, Pt. I (1928–36), pp. 71–81.

3. Oscar Albert Johnsen, *Nihundreårsminnet: Olav Haraldssons personlighet og livsverk*, 2nd. ed. (Oslo, 1931).

4. Adam of Bremen, *History of the Archbishops of Hamburg-*

Bremen, trans. Francis J. Tschan (New York, 1959), Bk. II, lxi (59), p. 97 and Bk. IV, xxxiii (32), pp. 213–14.

5. *Gamal norsk homiliebok, cod. AM 619 4°,* ed. Gustav Indrebø, iii, p. 114, speaks of costly gifts sent from the Varangian guard in Constantinople. For the donated silver cross, see ij, pp. 112–13.

6. See Ólafía Einarsdóttir, *Studier i kronologisk metode,* pp. 233, 235, on Snorri's sedulous research on chronological interrelationship of events. See also Halvdan Koht, "Kritiske undersøkelser i Olav den helliges historie," *Innhogg og utsyn i norsk historie* (Kristiania, 1921), pp. 124–41.

7. O. A. Johnsen, *Olav Haraldssons ungdom indtil slaget ved Nesjar 25. Mars 1016,* Videnskapsselskapet i Kristiania, Skrifter, II, hist.-filos. kl. (1916).

8. Marlene Ciklamini, "Grettir and Ketill Hængr, the Giant-Killers," *ARV,* 20 (1966), pp. 139, 143.

9. Despite Snorri's use of skaldic poetry, his account of Óláfr's role in the Viking army is largely ahistorical. See Johnsen, *Olav Haraldssons ungdom,* pp. 11–23; Ove Moberg, *Olav Haraldsson, Knut den store och Sverige, studier i Olav den Heliges förhållande till de nordiska grannländerna* (Lund, 1941), pp. 27–84; Alistair Campbell, *Skaldic Verse and Anglo-Saxon History* (London, 1971).

10. The political exposé includes a brief history of the dukes of Normandy and contemporary events in England.

11. This is ahistoric. Æthelred died in 1016, not 1012.

12. See Bjarni Aðalbjarnarson, *Heimskringla II,* pp. xcix–ci, who discusses the saintly virtues earlier sagas ascribed to Óláfr's youth.

13. Ch. 29, p. 36; Ludvig Holm-Olsen, "En Replikk i Harald Hardrådes Saga," *Maal og Minne* (1959), pp. 35–41. William of Malmesbury, *Chronicle of the Kings of England,* trans. J. A. Giles, Bk. III, p. 274, relates the anecdote to William the Conqueror's invasion of England.

14. See Edv. Bull, "Kong Olav Haraldsson: Problemer og arbeidsopgaver," *Historisk tidsskrift* (Stockholm), 50 (1930), pp. 145–48, 158–59, for the scant evidence on Óláfr's introduction of ecclesiastical laws.

15. See Bull, "Kong Olav Haraldsson," p. 148, on the lack of concrete evidence that Óláfr was a lawgiver.

16. Bjarni Aðalbjarnarson, *Heimskringla II,* p. ci, remarks upon the singular fact that Snorri attributes to Óláfr more cruel acts than earlier writers had done.

17. *Haraldssona saga, Heimskringla III,* ch. 2, p. 304.

18. This is territory that fell under the domination of the Swedish king after Óláfr Tryggvason's fall in 1000. The term *Friðgerðarsaga*

is applied to the conflict between Óláfr and his namesake, the Swedish king, and to the difficult peace negotiations. For a discussion of sources and historicity, see Bjarni Aðalbjarnarson, *Heimskringla II,* pp. xxviii–xl. See particularly pp. xxxi–vi, for the historic information conveyed by Sigvatr's "Austrfararvísur." These verses constitute the only contemporary source on negotiations between Óláfr and the Swedish king.

19. Elias Wessén, "Lagman och lagsaga," *Nordisk Tidskrift för Vetenskap, Konst och Industri,* 60 (1964), pp. 73–92, suggests that in the center of this fictive account on Sweden, Snorri placed the lawspeaker as a spokesman for freedom and order.

20. See Johan Schreiner, *Olav den Hellige og Norges samling* (Oslo, 1929), for a discussion of Óláfr's relationship to the aristocracy.

21. Ch. 219, p. 373. See also the hostile speech by the Danish bishop Sigurðr (ch. 218, pp. 371–72). The function of the speech (Lie, *Studier i Heimskringlas stil,* p. 101) is to summarize the points of indictment. This speech, though it contains truthful accusations, is patently unfair to Óláfr. The bishop's prejudice and lack of compassion foreshadow the harsh rules of the Danes (1030–1035).

22. Snorri makes it clear that Knútr believed he had inherited Norway, though he did not convey his claim until several years after he had won firm control over England in 1017. See Laurence Marcellus Larson, *Canute the Great 995 (circ.)–1035* (New York, 1912).

23. Some controversy surrounds the battle of Helgá (1026) (see Bjarni Aðalbjarnarson, *Heimskringla II,* pp. lxxvii–lxxix). Snorri creates the impression that Knútr stayed in Denmark after the battle and then conquered Norway. This chronology of events is incorrect. Knútr had journeyed to Rome in 1026–1027. He sailed to England in the summer of 1027 and left in 1028 for Norway.

24. Ch. 188, p. 340. This dream does not occur in any of the extant sources Snorri had used, as Bjarni Aðalbjarnarson, *Heimskringla II,* pp. lxxxii–lxxxiii, points out.

25. *Ólafs saga hins helga,* ed. Oscar Albert Johnsen, p. 84. The battle cry in this earlier version negates the concern for his people which Snorri ascribes to Óláfr. See Anne Holtsmark, "Kampropet på Stiklestad," *Maal og Minne* (1960), pp. 4–12.

26. Scholarly interest has centered on the discrepancy between the date of Óláfr's death (July 29) and of the solar eclipse (August 31). The sources also contain conflicting statements on the day of the week on which Óláfr was slain. The difficulty lies in conciliating or explaining the chronological calculations in the sources, calculations

based on the calendar of the Roman Church and on the Scandinavian practice of pegging the unit 10 as 12 and the unit 100 as 120.

27. See Anne Holtsmark, "Sankt Olavs liv og mirakler," *Festskrift til Francis Bull på 50 årsdagen* (Oslo, 1937), pp. 121–33, for the proliferation of legends and Andr. Seierstad, "Olavsdyrking i Nidaros og Nord-Europa," *Norsk folkelesnad,* 3 (1930), pp. 27–30, for parallels between the lives of Jesus and Óláfr.

Chapter Six

1. *Heimskringla III,* pp. 3–67. Magnús was born in 1024 and reigned from 1035–1047.

2. Ch. 9, p. 19. Johan Fritzner, *Ordbog over det gamle norske Sprog,* 2nd. pr., 2nd. ed. (Oslo, 1954), I, p. 278, lists *dýrð* as 'gloria.'

3. Interestingly, this scene is recorded only in *Heimskringla* (Bjarni Aðalbjarnarson, *Heimskringla III,* p. ix). Snorri apparently wished to demonstrate early in the saga the vengefulness which Magnús had inherited and over which he would later exercise close control.

4. For the quotation, see ch. 16, p. 31. Arne Bergsgård, "Skaldene um land og lands styring," *Festskrift til Halvdan Koht* (Oslo, 1933), p. 16, calls the poem "Bersoglisvísur" the *speculum regale* of the era.

5. See "Austfirðingafjórðungr," *Landnámabók,* ch. 364, p. 143, and *Viðbætir, Hrafns saga Sveinbjarnarsonar in sérstaka,* ch. 2, p. 378.

Chapter Seven

1. *Heimskringla III,* pp. 68–202. Haraldr ruled from 1046–1066.

2. Ch. 1, p. 69. For Haraldr's poetic skill, see G. Turville-Petre, *Haraldr the Hard-ruler and his Poets* (London, 1968).

3. Sigfús Blöndal, *Væringjasaga, Saga norræna, rússneskra og enskra hersveita í þjónustu miklagarðskeisara á miðöldum* (Reykjavík, 1954), pp. 108–68, and the bibliogaphical references on pp. 378–79.

4. Gyrgir is Georgios Maniakes, a well-known Byzantine general.

5. See also Johan Schreiner, "Harald Hardråde og Oplandene," *Festskrift til Finnur Jónsson* (København, 1928), pp. 157–72.

6. Per Sveaas Andersen, "Harald Hardråde, Denmark og England," *Harald Hardråde* (Oslo, n.d.), pp. 109, 115–16, 122, forwards a more dispassionate reason for Haraldr's invasion of England. Haraldr wished to establish a North-Sea kingdom.

7. Conversely, the chapter reporting the advance of the Anglo-Saxon army concludes with an ominous description of the armor: "the weapons glowed" (ch. 87, p. 184).

Chapter Eight

1. *Heimskringla III,* pp. 203–209, 210–37 respectively. Óláfr the Quiet reigned from 1067–1093 and Magnús the Barelegged from 1093–1103.

2. Ch. 26, p. 237. This motto is found in no other source (Bjarni Aðalbjarnarson, *Heimskringla III,* p. xlix).

3. The taxes abolished in the Trondheim and Uppland districts were the Yule gifts and the so-called "land-dues," to be paid to the king for the privilege of traveling or trading abroad. Chapter one and the beginning of chapter two are not found in Snorri's sources and are his own additions (Bjarni Aðalbjarnarson, *Heimskringla III,* p. xlv).

4. Ch. 21, p. 236. He died in Ireland on August 24, 1103.

Chapter Nine

1. *Heimskringla III,* pp. 238–77, 278–302 respectively. The sons of Magnús reigned from 1103–1130 (Óláfr d. 1116, Eysteinn d. 1122, Sigurðr d. 1130). Magnús the Blind assumed the rule in 1130, was blinded and deposed 1135. Haraldr gilli was slain in 1136.

2. The expedition according to Snorri took place four years after Magnús' death (1107). For the chronology, see Halvdan Koht, "Kong Sigurd på Jorsal-ferd," *Historisk tidsskrift* (Oslo), 5. R., V (1924), pp. 153–68.

3. The splinter of the Holy Cross was to be placed at the burial site of Saint Óláfr. Sigurðr deposited the splinter, however, in Konungahella. The archbishopric was established in 1153.

4. This account is not in Snorri's sources (see Bjarni Aðalbjarnarson, *Heimskringla III,* p. liv).

5. In *"The Oldest Saga of Óláfr the Saint"* and *"Legendary Saga"* this act of mutilation is ascribed to the mother of a later king, Sigurðr munnr (1136–1155). See Bjarni Aðalbjarnarson, *Heimskringla III,* footnote 1, p. 271.

6. See Anne Holtsmark, "Harald Gille, en sending," *Arkiv för nordisk filologi,* 77 (1962), pp. 84–89.

7. The sagas censure unanimously the two adversaries, particularly Haraldr gilli, for causing the precipitous decline in morality (Bjarni Aðalbjarnarson, *Heimskringla III,* pp. lxi–ii).

Chapter Ten

1. *Haraldssona saga, Hákonar saga herðibreiðs, Magnúss saga Erlingssonar, Heimskringla III,* pp. 303–46, 347–72, 373–417 re-

spectively. Sigurðr and Ingi assume the rule in 1136. Eysteinn, a brother raised in Ireland, receives a share of the kingdom in 1142. Sigurðr is killed in 1155, Eysteinn in 1157, and Ingi in 1161. Hákon the Broadshouldered claims a part of the kingdom in 1157 and is killed in 1162. *Magnúss saga Erlingssonar* ends in 1177.

2. The peace lasts from 1139–1155.

Selected Bibliography

PRIMARY SOURCES

1. Editions of Snorri Sturluson's Works

Codex Regius of the Younger Edda. Corpus codicum Islandicorum medii aevi, Nr. 14. Ed. Elias Wessén. Copenhagen: Einar Munksgaard, 1940. A facsimile edition.

Edda Snorra Sturlusonar udg. efter håndskrifterne af kommissionen for det arnamagnæanske legat. Ed Finnur Jónsson. København: Gyldendalske boghandel, 1931.

Edda Snorra Sturlusonar. 3 vols. Reprt. 1848–87. Osnabrück: Otto Zeller, 1966.

Snorri Sturluson, Heimskringla I, II, III. Ed. Bjarni Aðalbjarnarson. Íslenzk fornrit, Nrs. 26, 27, 28. Reykjavík: Hið íslenzka fornritafélag, 1941, 1945, 1951.

2. Uncertain Authorship

Egils saga Skalla–Grímssonar. Ed. Sigurður Nordal. Íslenzk fornrit, Nr. 2. Reykjavík: Hið íslenzka fornritafélag, 1933.

3. English Translations

HOLLANDER, LEE M., trans. *Heimskringla: History of the Kings of Norway.* Austin: University of Texas Press, 1964.

LAING, SAMUEL, trans. *Heimskringla: Sagas of the Norse Kings.* Rev., intro. Peter Foote. New York: Dent, 1961.

————. *Snorri Sturluson, Heimskringla, Part One, The Olaf Sagas.* Rev., intro. by Jacqueline Simpson. London: Dent, 1964.

MAGNUSSON, MAGNUS and PÁLSSON, HERMANN, trans. *King Harald's Saga: Harald Hardradi of Norway from Snorri Sturluson's "Heimskringla."* Harmondsworth: Penguin Books, 1966.

The Prose Edda of Snorri Sturluson, Tales from Norse Mythology. Trans. Jean I. Young. Rpt. Berkeley: University of California Press, 1973. An abridged translation.

- - - - - - - - - -

FELL, CHRISTINE, trans., ed. *Egils Saga.* London, Dent, 1975.

JONES, GWYN, trans. *Egil's Saga.* Syracuse, N. Y.: Syracuse University Press, 1960.

4. Editions of Other Primary Sources

Adam of Bremen. *History of the Archbishops of Hamburg-Bremen.*
Trans. Francis J. Tschan. New York: Columbia University Press,
1959.

Ágrip af Nóregs Konunga Sǫgum. Ed. Finnur Jónsson, Altnordische
Saga-Bibliothek, Nr. 18. Halle: Max Niemeyer Verlag, 1929.

The Anglo-Saxon Chronicle. Trans., ed. Dorothy Whitelock. New
Brunswick: Rutgers University Press, 1961.

Annálar og nafnaskrá. Ed. Guðni Jónsson. Reykjavík: Íslendingasagnaútgáfan, 1953.

Bjarnar saga Hítdœlakappa, in *Borgfirðinga sǫgur.* Eds. Sigurður
Nordal, Guðni Jónsson. Íslenzk fornrit, Nr. 3. Reykjavík: Hið
íslenzka fornritafélag, 1938.

*Byskupa sögur I, Skálholtsbyskupar. (Hungrvaka, Páls saga byskups,
Þorláks saga, Þorláks saga in yngri)*; *Byskupa sögur II, Hólabyskupar (Guðmundar saga Arasonar, Jarnteinabók Guðmundar
byskups, Jóns saga helga, Þættir úr Miðsögu Guðmundar byskups)*;
*Byskupa sögur III, Hólabyskupar (Guðmundar saga Arasonar eftir
Arngrím ábóta).* Ed. Guðni Jónsson. Reykjavík: Íslendingasagnaútgáfan, 1953.

Diplomatarium Islandicum. Íslenzkt fornbréfasafn. Vol. I, 834–1264.
Kaupmannahöfn: Hið íslenzka bókmenntafélag, 1857–76.

Eddadigte I, Vǫluspá, Hávamál. Ed. Jón Helgason. 2nd. rev. ed.
København: Ejnar Munksgaard, 1955.

*Eirspennill—Am 47 fol—Nóregs konunga sǫgur. Magnús góði—Hákon
gamli.* Ed. Finnur Jónsson. Kristiania: Den norske historiske
kildeskriftskommission, 1916.

Eyrbyggja saga. Eds. Einar Ól. Sveinsson, Matthías Þórðarson, Íslenzk
fornrit, Nr. 4. Reykjavík; Hið íslenzka fornritafélag, 1935.

Fagrskinna. Eds. P. A. Munch, C. R. Unger. Christiania: P. T. Mallings
forlagsboghandel, 1847.

First Grammatical Treatise, the Earliest Germanic Phonology. Ed.,
trans. Einar Haugen. Language Monograph 25, Supplement to
Language, 26 (1950).

Fóstbrœðra saga, þáttr Þormóðar, in *Vestfirðinga sǫgur.* Eds. Björn K.
Þórólfsson and Guðni Jónsson. Íslenzk fornrit, Nr. 6, Reykjavík:
Hið íslenzka fornritafélag, 1943.

Gamal norsk homiliebok, cod. AM 619 4°. Ed. Gustav Indrebø. Oslo:
Jacob Dybwad, 1931.

Grettis saga Ásmundarsonar. Ed. Guðni Jónsson. Íslenzk fornrit, Nr.
7. Reykjavík: Hið íslenzka fornritafélag, 1936.

Háttalykill enn forni. Eds. Jón Helgason and Anne Holtsmark. Bibliotheca Arnamagnæana, Nr. 1. Hafniæ: Ejnar Munksgaard, 1941.

Islandske Annaler indtil 1578. Ed. Gustav Storm. Christiania: Det norske historiske Kildeskriftfond, 1888.

Íslendingabók, Landnámabók. Ed. Jakob Benediktsson. Íslenzk fornrit, Nr. 1. 2 vols. Reykjavík: Hið íslenzka fornritafélag, 1968.

Íslendinga þættir (Egils þáttr Síðu-Hallssonar, Ísleifs þáttr byskups, Íslendings þáttr sögufróða, Þorsteins þáttr forvitna). Ed. Guðni Jónsson. Reykjavík: Bókaverzlun Sigurðar Kristjánssonar, 1945.

Landnámabók Íslands. Ed. Finnur Jónsson. København: Det kongelige nordiske oldskriftselskab, 1925.

Legendarisk Olavssaga etter Uppsala Universitetsbiblioteks Delagardieska samlingen Nr. 8 II. Ed. Anne Holtsmark. Corpus codicum Norvegicorum medii aevi, 2. Oslo: Selskapet til utgivelse av gamle norske håndskrifter, 1956.

Leifar fornra kristinna fræða íslenzkra. Ed. Þorvaldur Bjarnarson. Kaupmannahöfn: H. Hagerup bóksala, 1878.

Monumenta historica Norvegiæ. Ed. Gustav Storm. Kristiania: A. W. Brøgger, 1880.

Morkinskinna. Ed. C. R. Unger. Christiania: B. M. Bentzen, 1867.

Den norsk-islandske skjaldedigtning. Ed. Finnur Jónsson. 4 vols. København: Gyldendalske boghandel, 1912–1915.

Ólafs saga hins helga. Efter pergamenthaandskrift i Uppsala Universitetsbibiotek, Delagardieske samling nr. 8^{II}. Ed. Oscar Albert Johnsen. Kristiania: Jacob Dybwad, 1922.

Otte Brudstykker af den ældste Saga om Olav den hellige. Ed. Gustav Storm. Kristiania: Grøndahl & Sons, 1893.

Saga Óláfs Tryggvasonar af Oddr Snorrason munk. Ed. Finnur Jónsson. København: G. E. C. Gads forlag, 1932.

Saxonis Gesta Danorum. Ed. J. Olrik and H. Ræder. Hauniæ. Levin & Munksgaard, 1931.

[*Skálholtsbók.*] *Det Arnamagnæanske Haandskrift 81 a Fol. (Skálholtsbók yngsta), indeholdende Sverris saga, Böglunga sögur, Hákonar saga Hákonarsonar,* fasc. 1–4. Eds. A. Kjær, L. Holm-Olsen. Kristiania: Det norske historiske kildeskriftfond, 1910–11, 1926–47.

Den store saga om Olav den hellige efter pergamenthåndskrift i Kungliga biblioteket i Stockholm Nr. 2 4to med varianter fra andre håndskrifter. Eds. Oscar Albert Johnsen, Jón Helgason. Oslo: Jacob Dybwad, 1941.

Sturlunga saga. Eds. Jón Jóhannesson, Magnús Finnbogason, Kristján Eldjárn. 2 vols. Reykjavík: Sturlunguútgáfan, 1946.

Sturlunga saga I (Hrafns saga Sveinbjarnarsonar in sérstaka. Sturlu saga, Ættartölur); Sturlunga saga II (Íslendinga saga); Sturlunga saga III (Smákaflar ok brot, Sturlu þáttr. Svínfellinga saga, Þórðar saga kakala, Þorgils saga skarða, Viðbætir: Arons saga). Ed. Guðni Jónsson. Reykjavík: Íslendingasagnaútgáfan, 1954.

Sverris saga etter Cod. AM 327 4°. Ed. Gustav Indrebø. Kristiania: Jacob Dybwad, 1920.

Þáttr af Haraldi hárfagra, in *Flateyjarbók.* Ed. Guðbrandr Vigfússon. Christiania: P. T. Malling, 1860. I, 561–76.

WILLIAM OF MALMESBURY. *Chronicle of the Kings of England.* Trans. J. A. Giles. London: H. G. Bohn, 1847.

SECONDARY SOURCES*

ANDERSEN, PER SVEAAS. "Håkon Håkonsson den gamle for historiens domstol," *Nordisk Tidskrift för Vetenskap, Konst och Industri,* 40 (1964), 5–16.

ASHDOWN, MARGARET. Ed. trans. *English and Norse Documents Relating to the Reign of Ethelred the Unready.* Cambridge: Cambridge University Press, 1930.

BAETKE, WALTER. *Yngvi und die Ynglinger. Eine quellenkritische Untersuchung über das nordische "Sakralkönigtum".* Sitzungsberichte der sächsischen Akademie der Wissenschaften zu Leipzig. Phil. hist. Klasse, Nr. 109. Berlin: Akademie-Verlag, 1964.

BECKMAN, NAT. "Sverige i isländsk tradition." *Historisk tidsskrift* (Stockholm), 42 (1922), 152–67.

BEKKER-NIELSEN, HANS. *Old Norse–Icelandic Studies, A Select Bibliography.* Toronto: University of Toronto Press, 1967.

BERG, ARNO, ed. *Harald Hardråde.* Oslo: Dreyers forlag, n. d.

BERNTSEN, TORALF. *Fra sagn til saga: studier i kongesagaen.* Kristiania: Gyldendal, 1923.

BEYSCHLAG, SIEGFRIED. "Snorris Bild des 12. Jahrhunderts in Norwegen." *Festschrift Walter Baetke. Dargebracht zu seinem 80. Geburtstag am 28. März 1964.* Weinar: Hermann Böhlaus Nachfolger, 1966, 59–67.

BLÖNDAL, SIGFÚS. "The Last Exploits of Harald Sigurdsson in Greek Service." *Classica et Mediaevalia,* 2 (1939), 1–26.

* These entries are in addition to those found in the Notes. For more specialized recent studies, consult *Bibliography of Old Norse-Icelandic Studies,* eds. Hans Bekker-Nielsen, Thorkil Damsgaard Olsen (Copenhagen: Munksgaard, 1964–). For historic studies, see particularly the contributions in *Historisk tidsskrift* (Oslo).

Bø, Olav. *Heilag-Olav i norsk folketradisjon.* Oslo: Det norske samlaget, 1955.

Brodeur, Arthur. *The Meaning of Snorri's Categories.* University of California Publications in Modern Philology, No. 36. Berkeley: University of California Press, June 1952, 129–47.

Corbett, William John. "England from A. D. 954 to the Death of Edward the Confessor." *The Cambridge Medieval History.* New York: The Cambridge University Press, 1922, III, 371–408.

Cross, Samuel Hazzard. "Yaroslav the Wise in Norse Tradition." *Speculum,* 4 (1929), 177–97.

Fett, Harry. *Hellig Olav, Norges evige konge.* Oslo: Gyldendal norsk forlag, 1938.

Gardner, Thomas. "The Application of the Term 'Kenning.'" *Neophilologus,* 56 (1972), 464–68.

Glob, P. V. *The Bog People. Iron-Age Man Preserved.* Trans. Rupert Bruce-Mitford. Ithaca: Cornell University Press, 1969.

Gurevich, A. Ya. "Saga and History. The 'historical conception' of Snorri Sturluson." *Mediaeval Scandinavia,* 4 (1971), 42–53.

Hallberg, Peter. *Old Icelandic Poetry: Eddic Lay and Skaldic Verse.* Trans. Paul Schach, Sonja Lindgrenson. Lincoln: University of Nebraska Press, 1975.

Höfler, Otto. "Zur Bestimmung mythischer Elemente in der geschichtlichen Überlieferung." *Festschrift für Otto Scheel, Beiträge zur deutschen und nordischen Geschichte.* Schleswig: Ibbeken, 1952, 664–701.

Holtsmark, Anne. "Heroic Poetry and Legendary Sagas." *Bibliography of Old Norse-Icelandic Studies 1965.* Copenhagen, 1966, 9–21.

————. "Om de norske kongers sagaer," *Edda,* 25 (38), (1938), 145–64.

Johnsen, Arne Odd. *On the Background for the Establishment of the Norwegian Church Province. Some new Viewpoints.* Det Norske Videnskaps-Akademi i Oslo, Avhandlinger, II. Hist.-filos. kl., ny serie, Nr. 11 (Oslo, 1967), 3–19.

Johnsen, Oscar Albert. "Snorre Sturlasons opfatning av vor ældre historie." *Historisk tidsskrift* (Oslo), 5 R., 3 (1915), 213–32.

Kristensen, Marius. "Skjaldens Mytologi." *Acta Philologica Scandinavica,* 5 (1930–31), 67–92.

Larson, Laurence Marcellus. "The Political Policies of Cnut as King of England." *The American Historical Review,* 15 (1910), 720–43.

Lönnroth, Lars. *European Sources of Icelandic Saga-Writing.* An

Essay Based on Previous Studies. Thesis. Stockholm, 1965.

MARTIN, JOHN STANLEY. *Ragnarǫk. An Investigation into Old Norse Concepts of the Fate of the Gods.* Melbourne Monographs in Germanic Studies, Nr. 3. Assen: Van Gorcum, 1972.

NORDAL, SIGURÐUR. *Íslenzk menning.* Vol. I. Reykjavík: Mál og menning, 1942.

PAASCHE, FREDRIK. "Tendens og syn i kongesagaen." *Edda,* 17 (1922), 1–17.

SANDVIK, GUDMUND. *Hovding og konge i Heimskringla.* Oslo: Akademisk forlag, 1955.

SCHACH, PAUL. "Old Norse Literature." *The Medieval Literature of Western Europe. A Review of Research, Mainly 1930–1960.* Ed. John H. Fisher. New York: The New York University Press for the Modern Language Association of America, 1968, 255–80.

—————. "Symbolic Dreams of Future Renown in Old Icelandic Literature." *Mosaic,* 4 (1971), 51–73.

SCHREINER, JOHAN HENRIK. "Johan Schreiner, en bibliografi." *Historisk tidsskrift* (Oslo), 47 (1968), 6–13.

SEIERSTAD, ANDR. "Nord til St. Olav i Nidaros." *Nidaros erkebispestol og bispesete 1153–1953.* Ed. Arne Fjellbu. Oslo: Forlaget Land og kirke, 1955, 571–97.

SIMPSON, JACQUELINE. "Introduction," *Snorri Sturluson, Heimskringla, Part One, the Olaf Sagas.* Trans. Samuel Laing. London: Everyman's Library, 1964, I, vii–xxxv.

STENDER-PETERSEN, ADOLF. *Die Varägersage als Quelle der Altrussischen Chronik.* Acta Jutlandica, Nr. 6 (Aarhus 1934).

STORM, GUSTAV. *Snorre Sturlassöns historieskrivning. En kritisk undersögelse.* Kjöbenhavn: Bianco Lunos bogtrykkeri, 1873.

THOMAS, R. GEORGE. "The Sturlung Age as an Age of Saga Writing." *Germanic Review,* 25 (1950), 50–66.

TURVILLE-PETRE, GABRIEL. "Dreams in Icelandic Tradition." *Nine Norse Studies.* London: Viking Society for Northern Research, 1972, 30–51.

—————. *Myth and Religion of the North: The Religion of Ancient Scandinavia.* London: Weidenfeld and Nicolson, 1964.

—————. *Scaldic Poetry.* Oxford: Oxford University Press, 1976.

VRIES, JAN DE. *Altnordische Literaturgeschichte.* 2nd. ed. 2 vols. Berlin: Walter de Gruyter & Co., 1964, 1967.

WEIBULL, CURT. *Källkritik och historia, Norden under äldre medeltiden.* Stockholm: Bonniers, 1964.

WEIBULL, LAURITZ. *Kritiska undersökningar i Nordens historia omkring år 1000.* Lund: C. W. K. Gleerup, 1911.

Index

Names of minor personages and of most place names are omitted

185

186